MATURE THEMES

MATURE THEMES

Andrew Durbin

Nightboat Books
New York

© 2014 by Andrew Durbin
All rights reserved
Printed in the United States

ISBN: 978-1-937658-23-6

INTERIOR AND COVER DESIGN: Familiar
COVER ART: *Body Without Organs,*
by Alex Da Corte, 2013. Courtesy
of the artist.

Cataloging-in-publication data
is available from the Library of
Congress

Distributed by the University Press
of New England

One Court Street
Lenanon, NH 03766
www.upne.com

Nightboat Books
New York
www.nightboat.org

Even if the words, the fantasies, and the desire are all there, there s this awful policeman who is also there, alive

@Horse_ebooks

THE CANYONS

I once met a television producer who asked me if I had any ideas for a movie. We connected on the cramped set of a new reality-style sitcom he was producing for ABC called *Modern Family*. The director of the pilot introduced us as "two people who should really get to know one another" and praised us both for our work with him in the past. *Modern Family* is about the short-range social economy of a "non-traditional" family in southern California that remains close despite a variety of cultural interventions. Its politics are asymmetrical: the emphasis placed on the non-traditional in the family unit describes a program of normalization disguised as difference, making the show's central focus the slapstick of a self-subverting desire in queerness to replicate that structure more perfectly. Difference is translated into the reenforcing dogma of "family values," renewed (and concealed) by a "progressive" inclusion of gays and immigrants into its image of itself. It is always sunny and the comedy fairly tame, though occasionally the show touches on complex issues like gender roles, aging, and sex politics. This is how the producer described the sitcom to me. He never stopped smiling.

After the director returned to the shoot, the producer put his hand on my shoulder, squeezed it, and said, "Let's talk." He took me to a backroom, where production stored an outdoor table and deck chairs next to a grill, on top of which a rack of plastic ribs glistened under the halogen lights. He took a seat in a lawn chair opposite me and called for his assistant, who brought him a cappuccino but didn't ask me if I wanted anything. The cappuccino's foam swelled to the edge of the porcelain cup, nearly spilling over onto the little blue serving dish. The fluffed milk looked like the big clouds I saw drifting over the middle of the country as I flew to California the day before. The producer brought the cappuccino to his lips, paused a moment, then set it down after taking a sip.

"A writer like you," he said, "must have some great ideas for the movies, right?" I nodded. "Let me tell you the kind of thing we're looking for. It's simple. We want something fresh. Young. But not necessarily something for teens. It can appeal to teens, of course. We actually want that. Just not ... explicitly? It has to be," he paused to finally take a sip of his coffee, "it has to be something dark. Not too dark, right. No vampires, but still in the *Twilight* market, if you follow me." I thought about the *Twilight* market. He looked at me and flattened his tight smile into something like a frown.

"So do you have anything for me?"

I tried to put together my ideas in my head. Movies are immortal, I thought, but I'd never been sure whether or not Hollywood was right for me. Film was once our window into the present, "public consciousness" and probably the future, too. Now it seems television is the only worthwhile platform for the communication of real ideas. Could movies be that again? The clouds in the movies have always seemed more real to me than those on TV. There would be no clouds on *Modern Family*, that was certain, and I was not sure I could work in a world without clouds.

I looked at the producer. "I have an idea," I said, "for a film titled *The Canyons*."

The producer smiled. "OK. Shoot."

I pulled out my notebook and read from it: "In *The Canyons*, the post-Fordist mode of production has collapsed and its constituent parts have broken down under the strain of the resolve of those who oppose it and those who have worked to create new, virtualized alternatives exploding in the street. Nevertheless, their mechanics, and therefore the engineering requisite to dismantle them, remain permanently invisible to those it controls. Your beautiful, holographic face shimmers at the horizon with every totality that underlies my suspicion of your resurgent unity, despite what you do to contradict the burgeoning technologies that grapple with you. I've always had this feeling, almost always had this sense of the facts, that the importance of resolution over craft is one of the most important shifts in art making besides the creation of Photoshop and the invention of the death of painting. There is no plot in *The Canyons*, only its process and a description of the potential of this process as it scales the medium that subsumes you. While the network of these realities is limited, it is singular in its reinforcement of the so-called norm, under which lie the halogen lights that give every tile on the kitchen floor the ambience of a mansion in the Hills. Beneath those lights, there are only more lights. In *The Canyons*, everything is self-erasing and its only goal is to force its viewers to stare into its prismatic light until they lose focus in the digital assemblage that unfurls there, a total work in which Lindsay Lohan, the star of the film, is purged in flames and emerges as pure fantasy set to the dimensions of the tyranny of her infinite replication across all screens, on all devices. It is not the future. It is the present. It is a lovely, nostalgic music for a Hollywood we have dreamt of but never known. The process disassembles and returns to hazardous life as always, bringing you with it through its impossible survival. Eventually Lindsay dissolves or moves her hand to her face to pull it away and reveal her true self, the flat complex of appearances that manifests on the surface as a system of revelations that remain true even when proven false."

I bought popcorn for the usual price but snuck in my own soda. I went into theater 7 on the left and quickly found a seat before the film started. After a number of trailers for all the movies I couldn't wait to see, Lindsay Lohan's distraught face appeared on the screen, tucked into the wide light of the desert and the smoky wreckage of her Porsche. Her face was smudged with dirt and makeup as she crawled out from a roadside ditch, where her car had crashed after one of its tires hit a spike on the road in one of the desert's numerous obstacles that spares a starlet but kills everyone else. A few stray clouds gathered above her. The camera panned to reveal the empty expanse of earth while the light swelled around her and she summed up her future on the highway. She wondered whether or not she would die there, stalled halfway to Los Angeles. I thought about her famous quote: "Hopefully people will remember me for my work, not my car accidents." The screen went dark and the words

THE CANYONS

appeared.

I had read the film's synopsis on Fandango earlier in the afternoon when I purchased my ticket: Paul Schrader's new film, *The Canyons*, written by novelist Bret Easton Ellis, is a contemporary noir about the dangers of sexual obsession and the knots ambition produces in the lives of two characters, played by Lindsay Lohan and James Deen, a famous straight porn star whose substitution of an *e* for an *a* produces an uncanny transformation when you watch him "pound the shit" out of some blonde costar, erasing, by the audacity of his enthusiasm for fucking, any memory of the James Dean whose body exploded with equal enthusiasm in a car accident much like Lindsay's car exploded in the desert in *The Canyons*. She lives and he died. I thought: This is the film I have been waiting for, and ordered my ticket.

The Canyons is about a group of young people in their mid- to late twenties and how one chance meeting in the past unravels their lives, resulting in deceit, paranoia, and the cruel mind games that lead to ultimate violence, ultimate in that the slashing of Lindsay Lohan's throat closes the film. After the first scene, the film cut to the opening credits, then flashed back in time. Lindsay lounged in a blue tub, canopied by houseplants lingering off the edge of the bathroom windowsill. She ran her manicured hand over the edge of the tub, a gesture the camera zoomed in on. She moved her hand slowly, back and forth, letting water drip off her fingers to the tile floor below.

Producer Braxton Pope approached Lindsay Lohan's manager about the possibility of her playing a cameo in a new film by Paul Schrader, but during a meeting with Pope and Schrader, Lindsay said she wanted to play the lead. Two weeks later she screen-tested in the radiance of her very public decline and was cast as Tara in *The Canyons*.

Braxton later told a reporter for the *Hollywood Insider*: "She's very charismatic and she has a lot of acting skills…So for this part, we felt that she was really the right actor for a host of different reasons." Other actresses considered for Tara's role were Monica Gambee, Amalia Culp, Amanda Booth, Julissa Lopez, Fleur Saville, Lamorae Octavia, Houda Shretah, Larissa Vereza, Jamie Vandyke, Leigha Kingsley, and Ksenia Lauren. The casting director also expressed interest in French actress Leslie Couterrand, whom she felt had the look of someone who could "die gorgeously" in the desert outside Los Angeles. But when they brought Coutterand out to the Antelope Valley to screen test on site, she looked at the sand and refused to get out of the car.

Early on, the filmmakers considered casting Sean Brosnan as Christian, but when Monica Gambee fell through, they wanted to cast somebody more edgy and unexpected. Ellis, who in recent years has developed a strong interest in straight porn, had mentioned several times that he had Deen in mind for Christian's role. Schrader was reluctant at first to cast Deen out of fear that a curse might befall the set should they attempt to spiritually erase the ultrastar of the original James Dean in the course of the production of *The Canyons*. In the hope of assuaging the murky guilt that surrounded the set, Pope purchased Dean's infamous Porsche, dreamiest coffin of the last century, and hid it in a shed at an undisclosed location in Imperial County until the film's release. Deen went on record to say he did not share Schrader's concern, but that did not stop him from privately encouraging Pope to purchase the vehicle. Other actors who had been considered for Christian's role were Zane Holtz, Alex Meraz, and Daren Kagasoff.

When Gina's character was cast, the primary concern was whether or not the actress could work against Lindsay Lohan on-screen. The point was not to be ravishing but to ravish the camera in redress against its intrusion on their youth, Schrader said, and so they needed someone who could resist Lohan. A villain, more or less. After many auditions, Brooks was cast because she was overheard snickering at Lohan when she arrived on set the morning of her audition, visibly intoxicated. Other actresses that had been considered were Jenni Melear, Elizabeth Guest, Eline Van Der Velden, Spencer Grammer, Emma Dubery, and Jessica Morris.

When asked about casting *The Canyons* during an E! Entertainment interview, Bret Easton Ellis said: "Dealing with the casting of *The Canyons* was a great, liberating process—for both the production team and for the actors in general. We saw some amazing people that we will definitely keep in mind for future projects. The way the entire cast came together so quickly was a thrill and everyone who landed their roles deserved them. Using social media," referring to the Let It Cast method of finding talent online, "as a way to help build a film is really like riding the wave into the future."

Pope said to the same interviewer: "Nothing about this film was orchestrated in a traditional way. We wanted to actively embrace all the digital and social media tools at our disposal and give the film real cinematic value. *The Canyons* is the result of a forward thinking experiment with a terrific cast."

Schrader said: "Bret Easton Ellis's characters are beautiful people doing bad things in nice rooms. Lindsay Lohan and James Deen not only have the acting talent they also have that screen quality that keeps you watching their every move."

Youth is boundless. In this it resembles everything else. The future has erased the need for us to consider our bodies in terms of their need. I live in a chamber in the canyons surrounded by the screens that drift over me, broadcasting the faces of friends lost in whatever poor connection remains to bring us close, friends whose voices tend to my every whim, whatever they may be. I spend my days lying in the bath, though I cannot say who draws it for me. When I consider leaving this place I shudder and remember my happiness by pinching myself. Since I no longer feel pain, I feel nothing, which in things-as-they-are is exactly as I want them to be. I think about idols and the Venus who fell to the earth and was, for some time, rumored to live among us. Did you know her when she was alive? Do you recall seeing her across the pool in summer or has even that time relapsed and expunged from your memory the moment you later made eye contact at the hotel bar? Her smudged makeup cannot be restored; it too has receded into channels of a televised past, glittery in static, a face from which you cannot remove your gaze. The light is deep, every toilet seat pink. The weather distends any sense of time. It is only ever the best of summers, warm but cool. When it was hot, as it so often was, I used to lie on my kitchen floor, wondering when it would end. Now that it has ended, the present is soft and replete with pillows that surround you. I love my home, where everything appears on TV. And though you wouldn't have known it at the time, by the end of the nineties, this future was more or less ensured.

SMILE
ON A JET

going west, I look down from my Delta flight to California below, territory

of the imaginary in which clouds ring out utopias of the golden earth, rivers of milk,

rivers of excess that flow to Justin Bieber's "Baby," ringleader of the virgins

encased in his remote adulthood, he wears chastity like a veil to reinforce tween

sex appeal, which of course would be violated were you to touch him, oh oh oh

I cannot die I cannot be killed I can only fly across the surface of the continent below, landscapes of undying splendor and adoring peoples who shuffle en masse

to see me, everywhere, at once, hemorrhaging category of the straight male,

starstruck by the excess of disruptive totalities, bodies in a gym or smiling on a jet,

out of which, oof, their structuring comes in a wave, or as Paul Virilio writes

in *The Information Bomb*, "the smaller the world becomes as a result of the

relativistic effect of telecommunications," meaning Justin Bieber's Instagram,

"the more violently situations are concertinaed, with the risk of economic

and social crash that would merely be the extension of the visual crash of this

'market of the visible,' in which the *virtual bubble* of the (interconnected) financial

markets is never anything other than the inevitable consequence of the *visual bubble*

of a politics that has become **panoptical** and **cybernetic**," i.e., in bringing it

all together, the net of disarrayed particulars finally bucks the subjective field

in which a holographic Bieber moves, ensconced in his private jet, or more to the point,

the murder plot unravels but ends to reverse expectation and defers death across the event horizon, into evening, where the oldest man with a Justin Bieber tattoo

meets co-conspirator to finalize his plan to castrate and murder the pop star,

in a bunker where we regroup to arrange powers of attorney, flowers climbing up

the walls, my fingers close around the rail as I deplane at SFO, which is not

difficult though with an eye on the long view it might become impossible,

submerged in fog, going about for days, until I reach my advanced age,

in and out of feeling and deciding that, truly, the most beautiful place-name

in the United States is *Embarcadero*, Spanish for wharf, a place of departure,

I remember renting a van and driving around San Francisco at night, powerful

force of country music registering within its coordinates the activity of memory,

the split second at which I enjoyed seeing the word *Divisadaro* on a sign,

wondering what exactly Justin Bieber will remember of his travels, his name

which I almost wrote here as *Justine*, like the character in the famous porno

fantasy of the Marquis de Sade, prisoner of unsplit will, masculinity reinscribed in the supple dictator's body around which non-male-assigned bodies cavort

until twisted into the chain-link fence that surrounds him, the Marquis, writing

on toilet paper, Justine Bieber writing on his iPhone, a hundred wonders

that ought to be forgotten but not the alleged nude photos that prevail online

and his balls at the tip of a knife, such a different implosion of particulars that

makes up a night in San Francisco vs. a night at the Kids' Choice Awards,

onstage, splashed by slime as is Nickelodeon's custom, and to think,

even green goo, the texture of semen, became a corporate signifier,

Justine, Justine, I want to call out as I watch him drenched in neon DNA,

the purple sky above me untouched by the fog of the bay, so atypical I suppose,

but everything is not misfortune and with enough drive the speed to escape

this vantage point of the unholy world is enough to propel you beyond, into

the nonspace of air travel, globalized bodies of pop stardom, Thérèse beset

by misfortune, brought to the mud to make it holy again, the Madame de Lorsagne clearing Thérèse of any crime until she is struck, not by lightning

but by the moralistic literary device of a culture about to be wiped off the map,

I'm not criticizing de Sade I'm only suggesting this might be his critique,

so I head up north to the Redwoods, where, by the end of the twentieth century,

95% of the forest was sawed down to furnish us with a forest of the dead,

a ghost wood, the encompassing home of the lost brought together

by the crisp air of another day, my feet placed firmly on the spongy earth,

I walk with a friend to a tree where many people photograph themselves, likely

the most photographed tree in the park, into which I carve Justine, name

of our roseate exegesis and a totem, worthy of violation of the law to be written

into one of the members of the 5% as permanent fixture, the lonely forest,

the place I wish I knew best, which I cannot pass through with the speed

necessary to forget it was ever such a roaming territory, endless once,

a world of giants in which the living prevailed alone among the branches

NEXT-LEVEL SPLEEN

I went to my friend's house to watch a movie while her father was away on business in China. In her BBM to me she had proposed that we watch "something funny like … *Clueless.*" She made popcorn and whiskey sours in her dad's kitchen while I stood there watching her, my attention fixed on her hands. I had never seen someone make a drink so elegantly. She dropped ice into the Waterford crystal glasses and the little cubes clinked and flashed in the kitchen's light like big diamonds. She grabbed me by the arm and took me to her bedroom, where we drank the whiskey sours, took off our clothes, and made out while watching *Clueless*, visionary film that produced the frenetic self I embody today, adrift in the dreamier American auroras of endless summer. When the movie finished it started again and we watched the sky change. Pollution in the city produces the best sunsets. Tendency in the subject, motivated by spleen, to hate the urban conditions produced by alienation economic and social forces means nothing. I think I just love girls. She jerked me off and I came everywhere. Totalizing systems of thought. "As if," Cher says in the film a total of four times to vent contemporary spleen against those who misunderstand her. Get rich. Live life to the fullest. Destroy the world.

Later that night my friend said to me, "What do you think, is Cher an exemplary figure of first world mobility and the central conflict of the film is the sudden social intervention against her primary motivating force that she must 'win back' through alternative means, that is, as an automobilist whose privilege to a car is revoked and whose life is unshackled to the banality of financial concern of any kind, lack of car equals a death that can only be stopped via some hierarchy-splitting behavior like sleeping with your brother? Or is the film, like, an allegory for the failures of US ecological policy? That whole thing about the Clean Air Act and Wallace Shawn. Something totally dumb like that." She took a sip of her (second) whiskey sour and put her underwear and bra back on. She sat cross-legged across from me and smiled. I remained still and naked, thinking. "Also you look like the Buddha," she said.

"Paul Rudd plays her stepbrother ... and I don't know what that means. Are you, like, calling me fat?" I asked.

"No," she said. "I'm saying you look like the Buddha. Smart, you know."

I slipped into my form-fitting Calvin Klein briefs. The tight fabric felt good against my cock and made me hard again. She noticed my dick as it grew against my thigh and began to play with it through my underwear, laughing as I squirmed a little. I pushed her hand away.

"I don't think *Clueless* is an allegory for the Clinton Administration, with its various failures to respond to the emergent ecological crisis," I said. "Or any administration for that matter. Rather, I think that Cher is a flâneuse whose primary objective is to be carried through urban space without having to engage it herself. Like, no maps, just the directional privilege of wealth in which events and places simply materialize as though they were designed exclusively for her. Antiflâneuse, really. Like Baudelaire, who walked around but depended on his mother for financial support (like so many male geniuses of the nineteenth century) but updated for a culture on the cusp of GPS. Cher is perfect for LA's virtually unknowable supersprawl. Like, why bother? The central conflict of the film is not immobility, which, as you say, can only be rectified by some outrageous act against the traditional hierarchy. It is the fact that she does not want to go where she is going if she has to know how to get there. That was her original violation: driving around omnidirectionally without any attention to the regulating restrictions that give form to driving around in the first place. Stop signs, speed limits. Sure, she's only fifteen, about to turn sixteen, but not driving changes her position in the world such that she has to know how to get somewhere. Not driving allows her to give directions, to be picked up, to be taken somewhere. It's executive, easier—a non-problem. Sex with her stepbrother only paves over the problem of her position by eliding hers with his such that the unity of their relationship erases the issue that brought them together in the first place. Chauffeur becomes lover: all becomes one. Being a pop film, of course the act is watered down in that she sleeps with her cute but dirty stepbrother, Paul Rudd, instead of a blood relative, which would have been so much more interesting. But Baudelaire didn't sleep with his mother either, I guess."

"Um, I didn't need you to lecture me," she said.

"Urgh, I wasn't," I said.

I woke up late the next day in my friend's bed, but she was gone. It was the first day of spring break and she had gone ahead to the beach without me. She left a sticky note on the lampshade next to the bed: "Went to beach. Come!" *Clueless* was still playing on the TV. Cher was in class with the famous playwright Wallace Shawn. In my friend's soft pillows, I thought about Wallace Shawn and Deborah Eisenberg having breakfast together in Manhattan, saying things like, "Don't you think *The Times* made a serious error in its review of *Zero Dark Thirty*?" Wallace Shawn nods his head and sips his Nespresso. "I do," he says. On the TV Cher said, "Then I promised Miss Giest I'd start a letter-writing campaign to my congressman about violations of the Clean Air Act. But Mr. Hall"—Wallace Shawn—"was totally rigid. He said my debates were unresearched, unstructured, and unconvincing. As if! I felt impotent and out of control, which I really hate. I needed to find a place where I could gather my thoughts and regain my strength."

there are ghosts in Paris at the Place de La Concorde

       where Baudelaire still wanders for cash

you can't find them in the obelisk that encodes their presence there

       in his poem "Spleen" Baudelaire says the sky is like a lid

that covers the spirit. I imagine Tupperware for the soul

       unthinkable to Cher but not to the Home Shopping Network

ur-web of unlimited purchasing power

       revved in an engine of love

to perfect for you a home

       the pleasure of homemaking is so absolute

if not force in the network in the first place as is the assumption

       of both a soul and its container. Above me, the sky is the color

of the Home Shopping Network. In *Clueless* it's the same

       except it's also a blue that sweeps toward the ocean in undulation of wealth's confidence that it will go on forever

      in the lush Hills *Clueless* foregrounds

in "Spleen," the speaker is most disturbed to find any attempt

      to regain strength is necessarily thwarted by the endless natural

phenomena that surround him. Save the world and nevertheless

      it will skinny-dip in a malaise as white as midnight in Dostoevsky

everything is habitual and the soul denatures along these lines to find

      the earth and its pollutants describe a transformation

unstoppably beautiful, like, the world is gorgeous

      and I am gorgeous and you are gorgeous, even in the inky dark

even on the CalTrain, rising off the horizon

      surrounding us to form, as Baudelaire writes, "un chochet humide,"

or as Cher might say: a locker room of gross boys

      the fact still remains that the sky is boundless and rumbling toward us to unchain the light hiding below it, where light

    like massive beach balls

comes tumbling down to get MTV's spring break coverage started

    we can fully expect it will wreck us. But to return

to the Place de la Concorde, which is like a Venice Beach of stone

    without the beach, so imagine it's spring break

in Paris where Cher and Dionne dance to Kylie Minogue's

    "Can't Get You Out of My Head"

spring breakers everywhere dancing to an uptempo

    126-beats-per-minute mega hit. This is

what Baudelaire means when he talks about the world

    breaking out in a clamor of spirits or, in other words, sudden awareness

of the Big Other. I can't get you out of my head

    within the city walls music pushes forward to interrupt

this party, reneges any evidence of a despair in a frat boy's fraternité

      Baudelaire says the wind enters his soul

and like any porous category this rupturing is the conclusion

      that ends the poem but allows him to keep writing

why Cher goes on without a Jeep and what is referred to in the poem

      as Anguish or in *Clueless* as Paul Rudd

both drop down to plant a black flag

      (you can imagine Paul Rudd listening to Black Flag

while lounging with the Modern Library *Nietzsche* by the pool)

      into the poet's brow or to translate: the subject

acknowledges that in exteriorized forces

      the personality is determined by a variety of interventions that enter

the head like big symbolic flags in the conquered soil which

      seldom knows its defeat

um, but forgive me for puking, Cher, forgive me

for not whole-sale swallowing this bullshit

which is how Baudelaire begins

"To the Reader" the only contemporary analog of which I can think of

is "Niggas in Paris," boys' club of the privileged few

gilded among the *merveilleuses* and the lights

that have lit the city since 1881 against which millions

of Americans have backdropped among fireworks

avarice, all that, in the poor who in systematized

financialization of the body politic finally resemble

the nothingness that leaps up in Nietzsche to waltz toward

the end of the world at the home of Michael Bay

where we belong is ultimately the holy land, LA

Jeep-bound in the Hills

buried in the sunlight that illuminates

every face with the brightness that accompanies any intimacy

with death, even brain death

but what I truly want to do is be with you, Cher,

and learn to tell the difference between us

the intelligence of Baudelaire is anger with strategy

shovel off the world with boredom

to avoid work and its attendant wage slavery

heinous at the time of the composition of *Les Fleurs du Mal* shortly after the Paris Commune

which ended with its destruction

to create "youth culture," MTV

and its educational programming via MTVu

I'm aware that this has nothing to do with speaking to you,

dear reader, but isn't this what Baudelaire is talking about

when he runs up against the wall of the world

which encircles an obelisk of the world

standing in the middle of Paris it's like the word *incroyable*

a mouthful of revolutionary policy

like "ours" in Egypt

from which Paris imported the Obelisk of Luxor to the Place de la Concorde

a gift from the self-appointed Egyptian Viceroy Muhammad Ali Pasha

was constructed to exalt Ramses II

whose teeth rotted out of his head a pharaoh

whose reign lasted longer than any single French Republic ever has

nowhere to be found in "Au Lecteur" but its singular message as important

then as today: *WATCH THE THRONE*

never lost on the *incroyables* and *merveilleuses*

meaningless outside of some limited revolutionary context

which has subsequently absolved us of any need to be literate in its politics

who emerged at the end

of the reign of terror to infuse Paris

with the rare air of empire parties

fanning themselves with peacock feathers

gripping staffs wrapped in gold lamé

awash in a river

of luxury like a Bank of America exec in 2009

the pistons of the new world are pumping much faster, reader,

out of culture-bound mysteries

that rest here in the sun

while you, stand there still as always

antiflâneur or -flâneuse in memory of Cher

not singer-songwriter but the blonde

whose dusty complexion

mocks the world she faces to save

everything everywhere submerged in the moral philosophy

of "Niggas in Paris"

where the individual balls hard

in the exclusive right to be fair

self-determined in Paris getting fucked up

or getting married, as Kanye says, in the mall

no longer an important reference to the focal point of commerce at the end

of the nineteenth century but to every undergraduate

whose thesis quotes *The Arcades Project* extensively

in the morality of "Niggas in Paris"
like "To the Reader" it ultimately becomes itself
a teacup ethics to be thrown against the flower
wallpaper of the sitting room

reader, disengage
from the utopia of "my zone"
in a plume of desire
destroyed but alive, like you like me like blood

There is an infinite highway that builds toward Cher's Jeep. Everything is the pop gradient of Tumblr, even the desert in which the highway begins from our point of view. From our point of view the highway begins everywhere. Sunglasses and Advil, everything is mad real. For others, it begins with the faces of the dead, Ronald Reagan, Jacques Derrida, Gertrude Stein, mixed with the dust from which the road starts. Horizons mean nothing. Horizons mean the albatross has been captured and is dying, slung across the deck of the ship toward the teary-eyed sailors burdened by its bad luck. The procedure that envelops us culminates in a disavowal of the system we benefit from more substantially than we know. There is no other choice, art markets shift, make room for more art, then disappear. What is the light that springboards off the surface of a pool in the Hills? The white Jeep, pure symbol of wartime ingenuity married to lives of leisure, sits in the driveway and commands us to bow down. I was in awe as a child. I was in awe as an adult, too. Perfect suspension and a lightweight exterior both affordable and transmutable, the luminous soul of the entire project dwells there. A word that means so little and yet suggests the undoing of its own simplicity: Jeep. Two e's like in spleen, which Cher meant when she cursed her driving instructor for not giving her a pass. As if. Take away a car and you still have a passenger. I take walks everywhere I go, even in the supersprawl. Los Angeles, the antithetical capital to preservation, accelerates the speed at which we consume in order to perfect a place in the future as the site of the future. LA translates today into tomorrow by noon. But tonight, we can relax in the waterfalls of the Hilton as they flood with bubbles and champagne.

LANDSCAPES WITHOUT END

Clouds can archive. My fantasy is a landscape. Sometimes I daydream about merging my body with my computer so that I can more fully enter the landscapes of Google Earth, lush surface world without pollution or traffic, planet seen from the vantage point of space and roving surveillance vehicles, a motionless field, magnifying the normal imperfections and irregularities of the earth so that the planet is rendered transparent, misshapen and yet intoxicating in its languishing distinction from the real. Where are the palm trees swaying toward tonight? Standing at the beach nothing fails to come to mind, but out of blue prevalence thinking comes in waves. Am I my own vision? I am stretched beyond it, but beyond that, other oceans we hadn't known, lost continents restored in code. Where should we enter? The point where the digital camera clicks to record dusty boys playing by the side of the road? Weather in Google is fixed.

The night of Hurricane Sandy, I smoked a lot of pot, then looked at photos on Twitter of the flooding in the East Village, lower Manhattan, Queens, and Red Hook until the power went out, my phone died, and I passed out in my friend's West Village apartment. (News of Staten Island and New Jersey hadn't reached us yet.) The last thing I recall was another friend texting me to say that the city was evacuating the East Village in boats. Was that in my dream, I thought, the point where the present surpasses the expectations of history to bring about a future we were told we had propelled away? Windows blasted open. My favorite trees fell. The streetlights did not work when I was driven to Brooklyn two days later. This is what happens when you aren't paying attention and, over the hill, a car arrives with bad news, news that seemed impossible but in retrospect was the only news you could have received. I fell on a pillow. In my dreams I woke and found that everything west of 6th Avenue had sunk into the Hudson, which was now the ocean. I rushed with the others to the shore to take a picture. I stood on the beach where the last part of 7th Avenue remained, staring at the dark waters of the new world splashing up against the old one. I remember taking the Staten Island Ferry one night, the height of the following summer, and in a rage throwing my glasses overboard. I remember reading that anecdote in Joe Brainard's *I Remember* and thinking it was my life he'd remembered.

The prime directive of fantasy is aftermath. In *A.I. Artificial Intelligence*, the world is covered in ice, above which an alien species excavates the image of our future together. Our life in remains, trinkets, Coney Island, all of it submerged in water memory. There is no future that isn't also an excavation of some present. In *A.I.*, aliens float past the twin towers of the World Trade Center. In the future, are they restored? If only Stanley Kubrick had lived to make his movie. He might have known that climactic precarity is an economics of gloom, predicated upon a system of consumption that, in our lives, became a hostility normalized in time. In my vision of the future, the resurrected Stanley Kubrick reshoots *A.I.* as a second parable of the contemporary moment. Since every science fiction is a reading of the period that produced it, the new movie ends with the robot boy discovering that his only job was to promote the male family member, hobbled by impotency, to his symbolic function as Father—and not to love and be loved in return. The boy is abstract wealth synthesized into a Haley Joel Osment-identified body, the cork in the void of loss. The aliens, who have come to earth to find us permanently lodged in the landscapes we made for ourselves, do not return him to the dream of family life in which the mother's love is the focal point of his experience; rather they return him to the dream of labor. His mother greets him, then goes into her bedroom and locks the door. Landscapes are an economics. Toil over the earth as we always have and eventually it will toil over you. Will we meet in our mutual fantasy? Will I finally be your employer?

I once lived in a house in upstate New York owned by the disinherit-
ed son of the publisher of *Penthouse*. In the winter, the snow used to
freeze level with the porch, which was raised about a foot up from the
yard, creating the illusion that you could walk off it onto solid ground.
Once, a friend stepped off the ledge, forgetting that he wasn't walking
out onto our yard, and fell forward and disappeared. In those days, win-
ter was eternal. And I was the friend I'm telling you about.

In Los Angeles, I stayed with a friend who lived near a storage center for the Bureau of City Lights. When we walked to a nearby café, we passed by the fenced lot of the depot, which stretched an entire block. My friend suspected that it had been abandoned, but my friend is not always the most careful observer of his environment, so I couldn't be sure if this was true or not. I was struck by the huge array of lamps lying on the ground, a scene that felt like an incidental rejoinder to Chris Burden's *Urban Light* (2008) at LACMA. I read a news article recently about how LA is the city of the future because it is improving its mass-transit system. I think it is the city of the future because it takes the basic result of urban decline (i.e., decrepit infrastructure, abandoned buildings, deregulated public space) and uses it to propel itself forward. It plays its apocalyptic self-image against the plasticized glamour of Hollywood, producing a dissonance that one time gave me a panic attack while I walked through the public gardens in Pasadena with Kate Durbin. In this regard, one LA (there are many) seems to me designed as a science-fictional space, a patchwork of competing visions for how to structure our lives: into irrigated hills, domesticated flatlands, outer and inner social loops, transit brackets. In the future, the future will have ended, and the present will happen behind a velvet curtain in a nightclub at the bottom of Griffith Park.

In its comprehensive styling of known geography, Google Maps seeks the All only to find it cannot exist. Structured by the lack that a totalizing effort cannot contain, Google Maps is a matrix of fantasy and its correlatives, the between-space of representations of the real, altered and unaltered by Photoshop, a surveillance technology designed to render a fixed image of a changing field. In some time down the line, when certain landscapes erode beyond recognition, the most convincing evidence of their former existence will probably be Google Maps. I'm not a futurist except in this regard. Later, with a multitude of mapping technologies that will eventually render it obsolete, the original map will itself become a kernel of the real, distorting our perception of everything that we experience when we experience the so-called natural. Together we will watch the present unfold from afar. Glaciers, snowy mountains, fields: we will understand them only in terms of our seeing them represented online, consigned to the archive because their original, transitional form will have entered a delay between phenomenon and absence. I mean to say that these things are going away. Of course the bison we watch in northern Montana should graze free of our having to see them to know they had ever been there at all, but that isn't the case.

language is landscape

      every word dissipates into its mountains

      valleys and oceans

Laurie Anderson once said

virtual reality

      will never be convincing

until it has some dirt in it. This is also true for writing

base unit preference: the vowel over consonant

      consonants are buildings; vowels their foundation

vowels and consonants are organized

      into words organized into commands

language is weather, too. The water came up to 20th street

      and 10th avenue in Chelsea

      at the height of Hurricane Sandy's

storm surge

I played a drinking game until the power went out:

one shot of whiskey for every time

      the CNN newscaster said "surge." Thirteen-foot surge

drink

higher than expected storm surge

drink

the East Village was evacuated in boats

Long Island, Staten Island were partially destroyed

in the surge

drink. What does not change /

drink

You are fugitive. I am reverie!

No mistake is made without permission first. At sea, I have been this, with you, thrown into the pile of things moving across us in rhizomatic bliss. Do you remember the early passage in Joe Brainard's *I Remember* where he describes throwing his glasses off the Staten Island Ferry? To reinforce blindness with behavior, I return to this moment so often because I have thrown my glasses into the harbor, too. Melancholy, even in its most cloudlike state, is never invisible to others; it is only ever abstracted to its absolute and most potent normalcy until it becomes the environment you exhaust yourself in. Like taking a train upstate midsummer to be by yourself and finding that the entire train is full of people doing the same thing. Pollution is extradition of the everyday, detritus scattered across the mechanisms that create daily life in the first place. Joe Brainard washed ashore of this landscape, among the floating nuances of newly depleted resources like love, kindness, memory. How many modes of production can we fit into this sentence? Disaster is tremendous and overwhelmingly narrow in its concern. Can you name it? And does its name stick?

I once saw the city of the dead in Robert Gardner's *Forest of Bliss*, an ethnographic film about the Hindu burial practices in Benares, India. The city of the dead is not only filled with the dead, it is filled with the living who arrange the ceremonies of the dead, laying them to rest in the Ganges strewn with flowers. I saw this film a long time ago and can no longer remember what the forest of bliss refers to. Perhaps it was ethnography, the central point of the film being its silence—lack of commentary—and therefore the redemption of the anthropologist in Western liberalism. Perhaps bliss is the post-ontological lack after death, things like personalities hovering over the void. I watched bodies get dumped into the river as professional mourners gathered to say goodbye. Today the forest of bliss is on fire. And though I am not dead, someday I will be the flowering death that burns down the temple paying homage to it. Light of the country beyond me, in monsoon time, perhaps the forest of bliss will be a film that plays its demise then turns to ash, which we will stuff in our mouths. My death will reach everyone who has met me, whether they remember me or not. And my death will walk across the plains to the city of the dead to meet me in the forest of bliss, and together we will cork the void that is this mysterious landscape it demands.

In black swan theory, the event that disproportionately redistributes the weight of our attention—scales on your eyes, etc.—is always within a range of predictable options for the present but is usually unavailable to thinking before the event occurs. The new philosophers will spend their last days locked in their cars. It shouldn't come as surprise. It should come in Kansas, the ripple in the wheat of an ideology made of recycled paper. It should come when we make plans to meet on Saturday for a drink but cancel because neither of us wants to bother meeting in real life. It is easier to text than to upend the present situation, despite its roving paradoxes. There are clouds in my windowless bedroom. If I mention semio-capitalism, what kind of poet does that make you? Doze at the sight of its flowering, wear what is available, wherever you find it. Mercenary delight has already invaded the next world and is finally pushing back into this one. These signs point to the future but to nothing else, and therefore what do they mean? That when I finally bought a mirror I smashed it within minutes? Palms freeze, the world is covered in ice, aliens come from space. The future is traveling furiously toward you at incredible speed and will beat you to your destination to surprise you by its resemblance to what you have already seen. This is how the world works itself into a groove. This is why I chartered a plane, piloted by aliens, to see the city covered in ice. It was, after all, just behind a curtain I could easily part.

SIGHING FROM ABOVE

One winter, I bought a Tamagotchi angel in a Chinatown market. The
angel lived in a little plastic cloud made somewhere in an industrial
zone in Southeast Asia, quite far from the Chinatown I found it in. There
was a two-dimensional floor over which my two-dimensional angel
floated in front of a dark star on a camouflage-green screen. It was
made of seventy or so pixels that seldom changed except to animate a
bounce, a smile or frown, or a teardrop over its forehead, which signi-
fied that it was sick and dying. It wore a flowing robe, like the angels of
all the garage sale paintings my grandmother collects, and had a small
halo and two wings. My angel moved around its inch by inch screen,
hopping, shitting, and begging for angel food. I gave it a shot whenever
it was sick (it was always sick). When the little teardrop appeared at
the corner of its head, I had to toggle one of the three buttons on my
plastic cloud to retrieve the shot. After I would administer the medicine,
my angel would quickly be restored to good health, to holiness, and
so the small imperfection of my universe—the declining health of my
angel—was corrected until it shit on the floor once again, and I had to

clean it up using a separate but similarly enacted function.

After a few weeks, I started to think my angel had mixed feelings about being my angel despite my faithful attention to its every need. I had mixed feelings about it too, especially as my life became increasingly consumed with its care. I began to feel that my days feeding and tending to such a simple computer program of so few actions (sleep, eat, shit, get sick, die) were being wasted. If computers don't eat, why should a Tamagotchi? Moreover, I wasn't sure this was "appropriate behavior" for an adult. I had supposed at the time that it was a theological question, what's appropriate with regard to interfacing with angels, and therefore beyond me. I had very little knowledge of religion, but what I did know made me uncomfortable. An angel, made of light much like mine was made of light, led the only credible insurrection against the Christian God, until he too shit in his plastic cloud and was hurled into the underworld. Perhaps my Tamagotchi was a little underworld unto itself and my angel was actually the latest incarnation of Satan, our most famous herald of the Lord. I wondered if my tedium was some contrapasso earned in a life before a death I'd forgotten I'd suffered. The crude but nevertheless spitting image of an angel, the angel of darkness, the inverse of his earlier life in the upper echelon, the silver jet of a totalizing, incomprehensible power that hangs above us, like the sun, obtained in a plastic egg I kept in my pocket.

A few weeks after I got my angel, I rode the J train to a friend's apartment in Bushwick for dinner. It was the end of spring but the temperatures still hovered in the mid-fifties. In this refrigerated May, my Tamagotchi angel's behavior slowed down to a crawl, punctured only occasionally by shouts for food, for a shot, for a cleaning after it messed on its screen. My heater was broken so when my friend invited me over to dinner I figured this was the perfect opportunity to warm my angel up.

Angels eat so fast—nothing is ever enough. No matter how filling the meal might be, however complex (think about food as necessary fuel on the molecular level—but also as metaphysical splendor, food for the sempiternal kingdom arisen over us), it is never enough.

We watched the Food Network "for inspiration" while we cooked. Guy Fieri gnawed on the charred leg of a hog at a Texas BBQ. The meat industry is relentlessly excluded from our experience of its service: Guy doesn't show where the pig sleeps, but we can assume the machine isn't gentle when it handles her. My favorite chef, Gordon Ramsay, once said that someday restaurants will only sell atmosphere. In a reversal of his prediction, now that atmosphere is food. As a subject a hog is not atmospheric; in fact its presence is so excessively physical that it must be hidden from our experience of its flesh. Fieri renders it such in the theatrics of his consumption: the largesse of its death becomes a tribute to the life it gives, excessively, in the mouth of Guy. I stared at the TV while my friend tenderized the beef with a hammer.

I think you could fit this moment into a poem by Evan Kennedy, though he would likely reshape it into a wholly different poetics out of which one city might be posited against the backdrop of another, encircled in angels like wireless internet, the one I most want to live in, a kind of San Francisco of the sky. I am the most social animal in this city, I go from apartment to apartment for dinner and drinks, for sleeping around, for communing with the saints. But not to digress, there's this poem by Evan that I found online in which he writes,

> as I'm betting I'll make that
> heaven my home, and have an eye
> for it and ear for it, rather both
> eyes and ears for it and my own, as
> we're not opining that we'll stay
> these beasts,

I suddenly felt myself among those beasts, there in that unencumbered logic of dreams, years back at the Best Western in Savannah, Georgia, where I hid away for a long time and spent my nights and days listening to La Monte Young recordings and an audio file of Alice Notley reading "At Night the States" on repeat. In Savannah, I watched a lot of Gordon Ramsay, too. I thought about this gilded cult to which he belonged: the hovering system that coordinates the sexless angels whose lack of an anus indicates they don't eat, yet the presence of mouths, which I suppose are their right only as enunciation, all made of light anyway so what does it matter, suggests we might put a hamburger there and see what happens. I'm betting I'll make their heaven my home, some gold-leafed atopia linked by tramway back down to earth, below us the size of a blue M&M lost in black cloth. Do Tamagotchi angels have stomachs? I asked my Tamagotchi angel. I put my hand on my own to feel the movement within and confirm that I was still alive.

At the Best Western, the same where Paula Deen ran her first restaurant, The Bag Lady, I spent my afternoons sitting in a dark room, watching the TV glow with Food Network personalities at the center of the room. The living faces of America's top chefs smiled, hovered there, and I searched their expressions for signs of my own coming transcendence, for reconciliation with this tearful world. It was like going to church. The smell of Paula's fried chicken, then unknown to the rest of the country, wafted up from the kitchen below, and I often went to bed dizzy with hunger, the TV humming in the background.

There's a moment in the Oprah special on Paula Deen where Paula and her sons discuss the restorative effect of psychoanalysis. After pausing to praise Paula's angelic fried green tomatoes and sing to God, Oprah asks her to describe the schism that erupted between her and her sons before she became one of America's most beloved chefs. When she started The Bag Lady at the Best Western, Paula had recently separated from her husband and was seeing a married man. This infidelity, such radical divergence from the ethics of a Christian like Paula (born again or later, of course, and reframed as the necessary departure from the path to God in order to find it again), formed a terrible division between Paula and Son A, another chef, and Son B, the manager of the front of the house. To repair the situation, they went to family counseling, which forced them to confront the problem as one of positioning. The therapist asked Son A to kneel before Paula and Son B to look away, out the window, his back turned to the scene. The therapist then ordered them to accept one another as necessary to each other's happiness and to their financial success. The family immediately broke down in tears, left the therapy session, and was no longer sundered by Paula's destructive behavior. Together again, they never went back.

"How did this solve the problem?" Oprah asked.

The family positioning in the therapy session demands we read it in strictly Lacanian terms, substituting Lacan's famous triad of reality and our perception of it for each family member, the family itself being a patient of this analysis, Paula explained. In this session,

Paula represented the Real, the entirely constitutive but impossible to perceive truth that the family cannot see directly, or else it would explode in such close proximity to its inflexible horror. Son A, supplicant at his mother's feet, represented the Imaginary, that is, the component of the psyche that orients itself to the Real but which cannot look at it directly and therefore generates out of this terrifying knowledge the engine of imagination that allows us to cope with, and interpret, its presence in our lives. Paula did not look at him because he could not look at her—to do so would have annihilated the patient. Son B, lonely at the window overlooking the desolate parking lot of the therapist's suburban office, represented the Symbolic, the part of the triad that acknowledges the rules under which the other two are understood as components drawn together and united with him. Son B's pragmatic function as manager offers the consent to the law the family unit must give, despite the rough going of the back of the house and the inherent instability of the subject. In a sense, the Best Western was the Big Other, the symbolic order, through which all of this perceives itself as itself, rotating within its formative vortex that both lies at the center of all things and is all things. In the explicit structuring of the family as a single mind, the therapist resolved the competitive problem by forcing them to play the roles of the psyche that dominated each of them but which each struggled to master. I'll stay with these beasts, you might say, I'll eat forever until everything is made right.

Laughing, Paula told Oprah, "We knew we never wanted to go back!"

On my TV, Gordon Ramsay shouted at a woman who owns an unsuccessful Italian restaurant in Tucson. He showed her a thing or two about running a small business and about food, violently shoving the chef whose incompetence was the root of the restaurant's problems. Gordon is famous the world over, constellated among a curious society of individuals whose celebrity is predicated on a mastery of other people's desire to watch what they might consume without being able to do so. You might call them saints, carrying the desired world within them, disciplined into fame by its power. This network includes the illuminated kitchens of everyone's dreams, little churches and their patrons administered by saints of a demimonde. Magicians of flour and flesh, architects of houses of cake and honey drenched in crème and lemon filling. Gordon Ramsay said to the woman sobbing in her kitchen, "The beautiful is that which we do not wish to eat." She had just tasted her restaurant's lasagna and, sobbing, could not take a second bite.

Welcome to restaurant Gordon Ramsay the Prestige Menu today

will set you free Isle of Gigha halibut with Atlantic

crab finger lime and ras el hanout infused

broth no price listed

I assume pure

taste

so ex-

pertly prepared

unencumbered by

needless fat or oil Gordon will set you free

with Cotswold lamb and spring vegetables Navarin,

with wild and new season garlic pulled straight from the earth

in some mineral-rich soil no price listed but you'd pay anything

for Gordon I couldn't pull this off especially ravioli

of lobster, langoustine, and salmon

poached in a light

bisque, os-

cietra

caviar

and sorrel

velouté I mean purest

heaven spreading across the plate

no price listed to finish lemonade parfait with honey

bergamot and sheep's milk yoghurt sorbet all totaled $135.00

To dinner Paula Deen brought her world-famous Cornocupia Salad

Paula's favorite a bed of mixed greens para-

dise in garden vegetables carrots even

bananas a hardboiled

egg on top only

$9.99 for

an app

Shore is Good

Seafood Dip $9.99

speaks for itself shrimp and crab blended

served bubblin on toast points I'm literally falling

over myself for more until the fried okra served to perfection

only $7.99 battered and served up in a plastic basket for group

action with Paula's Creamy Chili Sauce even

an angel would kill for it I am starved

literally starved for

more shore is

good

I am

shouting over

everyone in the light

cast over the crispy flesh of Paula's

Original Black Pepper Shrimp $10.99 sautéed

in butter, crusted black with red pepper on toast I can't stop

Guy Fieri brought among us angels fine dessert from New York

cheesecake exceptionally chilled you can spot icicles

forming each one crusted in graham

crackers topped with

whipped cream

and sea-

sonal

fruit draped

across a bed of NY's

finest cheese encased in a deep-

dish cookie dough pie smothered in walnuts

you'll be knee deep in it for weeks baked in a sugar crust with a

mountain of ice cream on top leaving me in some fever of cake

in a bed of malted chocolate buttercream and Belgian

chocolate ice cream draped effortlessly

over double chocolate

layer cake

left

me

totally transfixed

urgh I can't stop Guy I could

pass out on a beach of fried ice cream $9

swimming in hot fudge sauce could you imagine

living forever, Guy, in heaven among angels frothy with delight?

After dinner, my Tamagotchi angel vibrated in my pocket because it was hungry. This was the fifth or sixth time it had done so in three days. I pulled it out and looked at its distressed, pixelated face, squared by a universe wired to hunger and a desire for my attention. "Please feed me," my angel chirped. After the feast we'd just had I thought it would be full for life, but apparently not. The angel Guy Fieri's fried ice cream left it only craving more. My angel continued to bounce up and down; its wings molted and folded behind its back. Long, silken feathers littered the bottom of the screen where it rested in a final malaise. I suggested to my angel that it eat and satisfy itself with the meat of Christ, but my angel shook its head and said, "It isn't enough." Around me, Chinatown froze at the still point of summer, the air held quietly over us, submerged in the complimentary aromas of duck, dried fish, roasted chicken, and pork buns, a disassembling zone of modes of commodity exchange amid weird silence. It was too hot to speak.

The summer my Tamagotchi died was the hottest on record. Its intensity relaxed by July into an oppressive norm I finally surrendered to. Shift in climate, fewer clouds, the trees do nothing. I missed my Best Western days, long before Paula's rise and fall, when air conditioning was a given. The summer my Tamagotchi died, it gasped before its personality self-deleted and said to me, "The difference between us is I can reboot whereas you cannot, you are evil, you surf mindlessly, you cannot PROTECT against bedbugs, you cannot reach your weight loss goal for just $4 a week, you cannot have infinite moments of intimate pleasure, you cannot congratulations you have been chosen for this special offer, get $10 and 6 months financing, work-at-home, you cannot make $7,487.00 per month without selling anything, it's brand new, and just about the most awesomest thing I've ever seen, the #1 easiest system ever for creating floods of cash from home, No Google, No Hard Website Code, no SEO or any of that other stuff, something totally different, you cannot start immediately, you cannot understand why this mail came to you. We have been having a meeting for the past three months that just ended a few days ago with the secretary to the United Nations, This email is to all the people that have been scammed in any part of the world, the UNITED NATIONS IN Affiliation with WORLD BANK have agreed to compensate them with the sum of $600,000. This includes every foreign contractors that may have not received their contract sum, and people that have had an unfinished transaction or international businesses that failed due to Government problems etc. Dear Sir/Madam, There is an issue with the WESTERN UNION MONEY TRANSFER PROMO in the amount of One Million Eight Hundred and Fifty Thousand United State of America Dollars $1,850,000.00 directed in cash credited to file UNP/90663/12 as 2012 payment, at the owner of this email address. This is from a total cash prize of $200,980,000.00 (US$ Two Hundred Million and Nine Hundred and Eighty Thousand US dollars) shared amongst the first fifteen (15) lucky winners in this category all over the globe. We found your name ANDREW DURBIN in the list of those who are to benefit from these compensation exercise and that is why we are contacting you, this have been agreed upon and have been signed. You are advised to contact Rev. Paul Jefferson of BANCO CAJA ESPANA of our paying center in Spain, as he is our representative in Spain, contact him immediately for your Cheque / International Bank Draft of $600,000. This funds are in a Bank Draft for security purpose ok?, so he will send it to you and you can clear it in any bank of your choice."

PRISM

At dinner, Katy Perry cried into her napkin. "It's no big deal," she said, waving away her personal assistant, who retreated to the corner of the room. "It's really no big deal."

"Why are you crying?" her current boyfriend demanded, turning to her. He forced a smile at all of us around the table, his first and only gesture toward anyone else at dinner besides Katy. She looked away from him. I thought the current boyfriend should chill, but he repeated himself, putting his hand on her shoulder: "Why are you crying, *Katy*?"

She shook her head. "I'm fine, OK?"

"*Surrrrrrrre*," he said, lowering his head toward his plate. He poked at his Isle of Gigha halibut. "Whatever."

I looked at Katy, who stared blankly across the table, just past my shoulder toward the shadowy hallway that led to the kitchen. We were at a dinner hosted by [REDACTED], a well-known record producer who had recently terminated his contract with Virgin Records and moved back to the city where his parents had raised him, where he had attended Bronx Science, and where, in college, he had listened to Madonna's "Vogue" and decided he wanted to produce other people's sound. A wax candle separated Katy and me. It had been dripping onto a plate of white asparagus all night and was nearly gone. The room was dark and the apartment evoked—at the muted end of the Bloomberg Administration, with its sleek, glassy high-rises—the sillier vibes of a haunted house, an older, vaudeville New York, gauzy with cobwebs. We could hardly see the food on our plates.

The producer's old Upper East Side flat had gone unchanged for sixty or so years, he had told us at the start of dinner. His parents died there and he "took over" shortly thereafter, among rumors of a breakdown in Aspen.

Katy wore what looked like several dead flamingos wrapped around her from ankle to chin. The birds' necks had been twisted to form a high collar finished in gold thread and little tufts of green fur. She had described it to me as "romantic couture" when we took the elevator up to the apartment together. Perry is gorgeous by nonspecific design, accumulating color and fabric without ever fixing a permanent look, except perhaps vague kitsch, itself somewhat chic. I tried to find the heads of the flamingos among the pink feathers, but if it ever was a flock of birds those heads were long ago removed, thrown away in the garbage, the necks stuffed and sewn up, tied and fitted to form the collar of the dress.

Katy Perry had just released her third album, *Prism*. It was, at the time of our dinner, number one and showed no signs of slowing down.

[REDACTED] returned to talking about his friendship with the boys of One Direction. (We had been discussing, among many things, American vs. British pop.) We all leaned in, Katy too, as he recalled the time he swore he saw two of the boys, Louis and Harry, enter the same bedroom after a party in Tokyo, holding hands, even though the boys had been booked separate suites. When [REDACTED] asked a member of their security detail about "the sleeping situation" the next morning, he said Harry never left Louis's room. "They can't keep their hands off each other, you know."

"They aren't gay," I said, turning to the woman on my left, [REDACTED], who nodded in agreement. She was the dinner's resident expert on American politics, but she counted pop music among her exceptionally broad interests. Her father was a senator and she served as a representative in New York's delegation in the House. "There's no way," I said.

"Have you seen them in concert?" [REDACTED] said to me, "How they touch one another? So gay!" He was solemn and a few people mumbled in agreement. Representative [REDACTED] finished her glass of wine and shook her head in disagreement.

"No," I said. "You need more proof than that. They're just being boys."

"Boys, all right," [REDACTED] said.

We were all very drunk. Some people turned to Katy to search her face for any hint she might know about the love lives of Louis and Harry, but she had already assured us that she had no inside information (throughout the night she claimed she was too busy to have friends in the music industry). In any case, she didn't seem to be paying attention to anyone but her current boyfriend, who kept whispering in her ear in an excited, somewhat irritated manner. Finally she frowned and waved him away, then turned from all of us to stare at a wall, where somewhere her personal assistant must have been standing in the shadows. I hadn't thought the star of the night would fade so quickly, but by the second course she was nearly gone: quiet, indifferent, distracted. Her melancholy rendered her a barely visible blue at the edge of the table where the candlelight dropped off.

"The proof," [REDACTED] said, mostly slurring, "is in their entire team, which is not only composed of assistants, producers, and other handlers, but also: a corporate mass electronic surveillance data mining program—known in some circles as DARK HORSE—run by a shadowy group of privacy experts who work at great distance from their immediate circle but who keep close tabs on them, and a number of other important celebrities, in order to control and manipulate their private lives, creating an environment of paranoia that ensures they behave on-brand and according to certain market-friendly values. Whatever they do is what gets out; the music industry—Hollywood, too—learned long ago that, in addition to controlling the media and its 'narratives,' they had to control their product on the most basic level, that is, on the level of their personal lives, by essentially erasing that privacy and colonizing what remained. This control ultimately proves effective in terms of curbing certain off-brand impulses, like, say, gay sex among the boys of One Direction, by creating a restrictive, fear-based culture of information sharing. Everyone lives in fear that their secrets will escape and alienate them from their fans, their source of income, and fame itself. Everyone knows that someone might know something, and so nothing changes."

He paused and made eye contact with me. I felt my jaw go slack.

Katy and the current boyfriend stood up. "We're leaving," she said. She turned to the current boyfriend: "Let's go."

"What? No," [REDACTED] shouted. He stood up, knocking over his glass of wine. A waiter hurried over with a cloth to wipe up the spill, but [REDACTED] pushed him out of the way. Katy and the current boyfriend exited the dining room, flamingo feathers peeling off as they rushed to the door. The personal assistant trailed behind them, texting the driver below to ready the car. (She kept yelling: "Texting the car, texting the car!") [REDACTED] followed them into the vestibule where they stood waiting for the elevator. Everyone at the table leapt up and moved to the hallway that led to the scene. I gathered the feathers in the dark as I moved toward the front of the apartment, where our host was frantically pleading with Katy not to go. "I was just kidding," he said.

"No," said the current boyfriend. "This is so fucking ridiculous." Katy said nothing and didn't look at anyone. When the elevator arrived, she stepped into it and flashed us the middle finger.

"Fuck you," the current boyfriend said as the elevator doors closed.

Katy Perry's *Prism* begins parade-like with "Roar," soundtrack to historical remainders rediscovered on other shores, locked in the purple light of Audis on the beach or among south Florida palms on Ocean Drive, getting fucked up on the beach, getting like really fucked up on 5-Hour Energy, recoiled in glassy rainbows rising out of the sea. Katy Perry makes me feel like I'm high in the mall or tripping on GHB in a public pool. Days rendered speechless with my hair full of sand, all this blond hair full of sand and I can't stop: "Dancing through the fire cause I am the champion and you're going to hear me roar." Like really, I can't stop. It begins a thing flittering behind the system at present, idiotically beautiful in its neon glow, the revolutionary agent of a social life made to bloom at gunpoint into something-ness, dizzying, embers left of the Members Only jacket burned at the bonfire. It is endless and somewhere there is a phrase to describe it that will come to me. I suppose it's a ball. I suppose it could be something else, too. In *Prism*, everything is leveled by a pop indifferent to individuated life. Love is everywhere and nowhere at once. It renders the varieties of experience singular, sucking it all in: flattened, affectless, and blissed out like a night spent drinking on Venice Beach. Katy's music is a mutant pop, collating genre without ever assuming the pose of a stable POV. Only "Dark Horse," which begins with a high-pitched "oh no" before it descends below the stadium benches at the high school football game to romance taken up among the shadows, Eros made cosmic in its troubled gorgeousness, suggests any configuration outside the usual boy-girl love, boy-girl breakup, boy-girl regret, boy-girl makeup. "Make me your Aphrodite, your one and only. Make me your enemy," she sings. Later:

Juicy J raps, "She eat your heart out like Jeffrey Dahmer"—a necrophiliac cannibal who murdered, dismembered, and consumed seventeen boys in the 1980s—before he reverts (as the album often does) to cliché: love is an addiction. But is Katy addicted to dismembering and eating her lovers? In her America, which closely resembles everyone else's, we love fuck party live forever, even if living forever happens to be terminally cliché: "All we have is this moment," "They say one man's trash is another man's treasure." It is a feeling that organizes other feelings into one feeling that describes only itself: an ocean of nostalgia that I love to swim in.

The dinner party followed them down in the next elevator. When we arrived outside of the apartment, Katy stood on the sidewalk, waiting for her driver to pull up.

"Katy, Katy," [REDACTED] said. She looked at each of us, moving her eyes from face to face, but said nothing. Her current boyfriend moved forward to block our host from getting any closer.

"Hey, man," he said, "I, like, really need you to step the fuck back."

"No, no, I understand," he said, "I just don't see why you have to leave. I am happy to apologize. I am *sorry.*"

"Sorry won't cut it, asshole," Katy said. I stared at her neck in the streetlight to see if I could finally make out the heads of the flamingos wrapped into the collar, but I still couldn't see any of them. Our host tried to approach Katy and the current boyfriend, but the current boyfriend stepped up and pushed him back.

"Man, I told you to step back," he said.

From around the corner, a Bentley pulled up and stopped at the entrance to the building. A driver stepped out and opened the door for them. She frowned at us before entering the car. I watched her slide into the heavenly seclusion of its leather interior. The driver shut the door. [REDACTED] began to knock on the window. The driver immediately yanked him back by his shoulder. "Touch my car again, buddy, and I'll break your fucking hand."

"OK, OK," he said, and stepped back, putting his hands in his pockets.

The driver nodded and got into the car. They drove off.

Katy's sudden absence felt oceanic. But when I looked at it, at the vacant, shadowy 72nd Street, I saw nothing, neither the other dinner guests nor the car as it began to turn onto Lexington. I saw nothing that would allow me to define "ocean," as in the biological and ecological contingency that has come to mean "ocean," let alone "absence." This, like other things, was OK, even a little nice. *Prism* is itself an ocean of feeling. Its waves quiver under a moon the shape of Katy's transformative, prismatic face ebbing in the dark, haloed in blue.

Your ocean is flowing toward me, Katy, I thought, as I stood under the canopy of a palm tree at the empty shore, which wasn't so much a palm as it was a pun on the fist unballed before a reader who began to trace its creases. He ran his fingers along the groove of my palm, searching the revelatory lines that have crossed one another to locate the coordinates of some future rapidly becoming present.

I asked him what it meant, but he just shook his head.

I looked at him and tried to understand what this might mean, but he didn't seem to know. He sat at his desk and sighed, looked at his computer screen, and transferred information he located in several databases into a few Excel spreadsheets open on his desktop in preparation for an extended memo due at the end of the week. His chair squeaked and he wrote a Post-it note to remind himself to tell head of operations that he needs a new chair. He occasionally looked at the clock near his outgoing mailbox. As always, he felt "stretched thin."

He often wondered if his coworkers were as bored as he always was. He doesn't have an office window to look out of but he frequently likes to pause in his day to imagine what is outside the building: the parking lot, the road that leads out of Virginia and back to D.C. He finds this life theoretically beautiful though in practice he could see himself doing other work. That other work remains unknown in its details to him but he thinks about what it could be fairly often. It would be something practical but beautiful.

Whenever the song "Dark Horse" plays on his iPod shuffle, the reader thinks about suggesting that title as a name for a program the office—or rather, the complex of agencies collated into what he refers to as "the office"—is developing. The song, like the other songs on the album, reminds the reader of a time he had dinner with a high school girlfriend's parents, the night of a significant local football game. Her father was an intolerant man who, after 9/11, found a vital resource for his hatred in the internet. Her father peddled in conspiracies related to the complicity of the Bush Administration in designing and executing the attacks, which he cryptically referred to as "the Opening." He would often begin sentences: "Before the Opening" or "After the Opening." The Opening, as he described it to the reader, was the event that both admitted the veracity of the lie and the falsity of the truth simultaneously; that is, the Opening articulated two points about reality, holographic in its lush, simulated surfaces: one, that the perceivable conditions of life in the United States were lies that covered up the generators of those conditions and, two, the lies preempted what created them and so remain the primary "reality" (and not, as shadier conspiracies might have it, the reverse). He liked to say that facts were useless things. What matters is the dream that gives those facts a purpose, a life.

After that dinner, the Opening became a frequent reference point for the reader as he left his hometown, attended Georgetown, and began to work in the DC metropolitan area. He often thought about its merits and debated it with himself privately. Soon the reader began to feel the Opening everywhere, at every instance, whether he was at work or at the gym or having a drink or listening to *Prism*, which he gradually discovered (as he discovered with many, many things) was based on this exact twinned point. Perry puts it more simply, the reader thinks, in arguing that the fantasy that renders the present experiential does not conceal a "deeper," more "true" reality. Rather, it is fantasy that allows reality to spread.

He leaned back in his chair. It squeaked under his weight.

"Dark Horse" evokes the early Sunday hours at the height of the American weekend, the last minutes before sunrise, when you either choose among the dazed remnants of the night or go home alone. Also, the highly organized systems of information management that cache, tag, and categorize both the metadata of these remnants (text message: "hi what r u doing rite now its late i know"; recorded as "Message containing no flagged content sent at 3:02:42AM 11/08/13 from Maison O, 98 Kenmare Street, New York, New York 10012) and the remnants themselves (recorded as: ANDREW SCOTT DURBIN, resident of 855 Park Place, Brooklyn, New York 11216; born 09/28/89; profile clear of flagged content. SEE MORE). The cover of Perry's *Prism* features a photograph of the artist taken by Ryan McGinley, whose terrible work effaces the marks of aging and those that differentiate youthful bodies by reducing them to a blur, blotched in the sunlit fields or the caves out west, flakes of flesh tones in which only the vaguest outline of a thin college student emerges, naked, unseduced by the camera itself but in love with the audience at the other end of the process that manufactures his image. People stare at them in the gallery or scrolling through a blog on their iPhone, the faces staring back, sometimes very clear, sometimes still blurrier, prismatic, triangulated as viewer, model, and the networks of distribution for which Ryan McGinley serves as a conduit for an idea of beauty not exactly universal as it strives toward a uniqueness defined by the unexpected intensity of the sight of someone's sharp pelvis or high cheekbones but getting there. They are strange, even ugly in McGinley's photographs, and yet this doesn't deprive them of their magnetism. The three of us—model, Ryan, and I—begin to organize into a record of taste to be graphed by agencies more or less invisible to us. I text my friend "hi what r u doing rite now its late i know" and even though I am certain no response will come I go deep and send it again. The impulse is, itself, based on a belief in the dark horse: that a thing probably won't happen leads me to think that it must. In [REDACTED]'s apartment, everything darkened as we resumed our places at the table. In the candlelight, I stared at the cover of Katy's new album, narrowing in on the little A in Katy shaped like a triangle, a prism, over Ryan McGinley's sun-drenched image of her as she catches the light, and it became easy to see in it another prism, lying in repose among the sunflowers, the quartz pyramid through which light becomes a rainbow or in other iterations, rectangular or cubic or pentagonal or, finally, the hexagonal crystal, in which I see myself telling Katy to back up a step, please, Katy, can someone get her some makeup please? and raise the silvery cloth up to your lips before the green screen where my assistants later overlay the field that seems real but probably isn't, or back of that, another prism that spins in a nest of light, tagging content endlessly, storing that content into the plural databases where I take residence among the machines who read me, who render me legible in various other systems languages, flagging "bomb," for example, like, Katy Perry is the bomb, Katy, you're the bomb, as the prism spins in my hand and I bring it close to speak into it, pressing it to my lips, under a prismatic sunset a gradient of red like the stroked, reddish brown hair of a horse moving across a field, the field where the sunflowers do not wilt under the hand of Ryan McGinley's assistants, the horse moving quickly through it, running up and turning back at the electrified fence over and over again in a game it plays with the only environment it knows. I raise my phone to take a picture. I hold it close, tap the screen to focus the image, but the horse moves too quickly and I only manage to snap a photo of a blur. I post it to Instagram anyway, marking for friends and the servers mainlined to the various agencies that might take note that, somewhere, I saw a horse, and that that horse was moving fast.

SIR DRONE

Raymond Pettibon writes on Twitter: "Art will recover from its low self-esteem vis-à-vis other 'disciplines' when artists are recruited by the CIA—as they were in the 50's(smile)." For a second I wonder if the parenthetical smile suggests Pettibon has secret information about artist spies or if he himself was an artist spy in the 1950s, but since he was born in 1957, I credit the tweet to the usual spooky disposition of his Twitter, where he often writes conspiratorially about GG Allin, sports, punk rock, art, violence, and politics, using a prose style notable for its confusing grammar, atypical punctuation, and eccentric choices in spelling— especially in his use of the letter Y, which manifests virally where it never belongs, populating words with an extra vowel/consonant that often confuses their sense-meaning. His father wrote spy novels and writing—a fundamental component to his work—"came natural" to him, as the *Los Angeles Times* wrote about the 33 year-old Pettibon in 1991. They described him as having a boxer's nose, and if I were to describe him now I'd say the same thing. We both live in New York and sometimes I think I might run into him. I went to his 2013 show at David

Zwirner in Chelsea with my friend Ed several weeks after it opened and impossibly expected him to be there, but of course there was no way he'd be at the gallery on that day—or on any day, for that matter. I can't really place why seeing his work imposes his presence or the possibility of his presence on me. I suppose it's the largeness of his personality, in his art and on Twitter, that makes me think he lives in every space where you find him, Y-like—edged with the sense that he could be there just as easily as he could not be there. Pettibon, in portraits of him then and now, looks a little wrecked by whatever world he does occupy, dreamless on the green lawns of a vague yesterday or, since he lives in New York, cast in the shadowy Real of the monumental skyline, each platform of being-there more confused than the next in the poignancy of its crumbling under certain inescapable brutalities like those he illustrates. In Pettibon's drawings, there is defeat with no recourse to recovery of self-esteem. At his David Zwirner show, I thought about how his art stretches bodies thin, into a vocabulary of bodies that exposes an emotional interior usually secluded in the flesh, itself (the bodied body) a dominant narrative through which we discover their point, which is: we try to destroy ourselves but survive, as always, flatlined then brought back only to be measured for life by an entirely different system of measurement than one previously known. Like his Twitter, like the trippier poetry of a language constantly on the verge of discovering at its heart a vulnerability so substantial as to be meaningless, his art attempts to recover its low self-esteem vis-à-vis an engagement with fragility—with fragile bodies. Also with language itself, which stretches along the paper in Pettibon's slanted sprawl, corrupted by misplaced Y's, like in the line "WHAT WE CANN NOYT STOYP TO ILLUSTRATE WE MUST PASS OVER IN IGNORANCE," a misquote of Wittgenstein, written in blue watercolor on toilet paper and pinned to the wall at David Zwirner. On the other side of the room, Ed looked at a large wave under which Pettibon had written: "TO BE WIPED OFF THE FACE OF THE EARTH—NOT WITHOUT A PICTURE FIRST." Two men lose their surfboards in the midst of the huge curve, and though they've been flattened into a stasis indispensible from the work's effect I thought Ed seemed a little dizzy from the hugeness of the drawing and the feeling of it crashing down on him. Or perhaps, after a night out, I felt a little dizzy in the midst of so many uncrashed waves and when I looked at Ed I thought he must have felt small, like I felt small, under that frozen wave. It's like wandering out into the ocean, to the point where the waves are so large that you have to duck down into the water to withstand their arrival at shore. Otherwise you're knocked back with a mouthful of salt water. I recently read in a science magazine that the world transformed by inhospitable shifts in climate will be taken over by jellyfish, which is the most adept of any of us at handling an ocean at higher temperatures and decreased salinization. One night at the beach in southern California, I discovered in the waves this other, future ocean captive within the one at present, glittery in the vacuum of its false glamour, suggesting in the cloud of bright jellyfish glowing at the crest of each wave a coming world hallucinogenic in its gelatinous light, droning at sea, curtained in my presence by a diffuse electric air. It was unremarkable by nature, a zone relinquishing its hold on actual space, curtailed by boundaries that self-effaced, a residual empire of presence that wandered away, dissipating, but not without leaving behind the possibility of later return—as the whole world. I felt taxed of the energy to place myself within it, like thinking California might be different from any other place not-California, blasted into the continent, woods and oceans, resorts and plazas. In other works of Pettibon's, Y's rise into the language to interrupt meaning: increasing redundancy where it might be reduced, all over the walls and in the drawings, to a terse language that spells out hardship. Life fucks with people on a basic, immaterial level, leveling charges against them that float dreamily over or under the subject. A man running away: "I THOUGHT CALIFORNIA WOULD BE DIFFERENT." A man stabbing another: "YOUR GIRLFRIEND CALLED ME CHICKEN." A man and woman kissing: "I DON'T LOVE YOU ANYMORE." A cat that has killed a rat: "I HAVE KILLED HIM FOR YOU, AND I'VE BROUGHT HIM TO YOU AS A REMINDER OF OUR OWN INEVITABLE SLIP INTO THE GREAT NOTHING." Sobered by language, they hunch over or hold on to the most straightforward things, the things most immediately and obviously present, even if present things never settle down. A basketball player holds a gun and a ball: "DO YOU MIND IF I DUNK?" The white gallery, at one moment, became a lilac cube with me at its center, draped in the sleepier gradient of a late Saturday afternoon in fall. I imagined the basketball player standing beside me, loading the gun. A few nights later, Ed WeTransferred me *Sir Drone*, one of four of Pettibon's VHS tapes he made in the 1990s, a film that stars Mike Kelley as a would-be punk rocker named Jinx trying to start a band called the Droners with his friend Dwayne. I WeTransferred the file to Zachary four days later while he was at work. Rather, I forwarded the WeTransfer Ed sent me to Zachary and asked him if that worked and it did. In her poem "Orange Roses," Lucy says that she lent Zachary—the same Zachary—a book that she doesn't expect to get back, though he returns it a month later. I am thrilled that I can lend him something and never worry about its return since its life in the cloud totally absolves us of all the guilty lender/borrower feeling of when should I ask for it back? when should I give it back? economy that's totally a drag. It's the same drag Jinx and Dwayne feel as they try to start a band and learn the complex vocabulary of punk rock, a visual and linguistic system that requires a certain aping with confidence, borrowing from it here and there, unsure of what, and how, to give back. I feel that. Friendship gets meted out in blood: Jinx and Dwayne give each other prison tattoos and generally bromance like men in that kind of love. They also struggle to erase whatever residual uncool defines their read of one another, like hippiness (bell bottoms are torn) and surfing (a swastika'd surfboard is threatened to be sold). Mike Kelley seems to feel it in his bad acting, which rises Y-like to a reality unexpected but obviously the only one we could have in the videotape, now a digital file, playing on my VLC app. It's the reality pressurized as a matter of active endurance rather than passive enjoyment. Performance excites it all back to life. It's a good movie but so what. When I watched it, *Sir Drone* was like a caption, only it captioned me: I THOUGHT THIS WOULD BE DIFFERENT. But how? Better? I guess in 2013 the title *Sir Drone* reminded me of the semisecret paramilitary US drone campaigns in Yemen and Pakistan. Or, combined with that, Stevie Wonder's "Sir Duke." Perhaps "Sir Duke" plays in the command center that signals a drone to strike a bus. I tried to imagine what it would be like if the Droners covered "Sir Duke." It might sound better than the original,

which, to be heretically frank, is a little too cute in its uppercase impera-
tive to enjoy, solidified to a taffy-like mask stretched over my face, my
face which at the Pettibon show felt masked as I stared at his drawings.
Outside the gallery, the sky went dark. I parted with Ed and walked
south, down into the Village, to wander around alone. The Chelsea
streets were cold, cast partially in the purple light of a Porsche with LED
Underbody lights installed to its bottom frame that I passed below 14th.
A few wasted bros gathered on 9th Avenue to admire the car, which
seemed more like an illustration of a car than an actual one. I was
impressed by the unchallenged brightness that swamped us, a little
unworldly in its puce spray across the sidewalk, just north of the
Standard Hotel, where some high-net worth individuals congregated
near the entrance, among them maybe even the owner of the Porsche. It
sat in the street like a big, luxurious coffin. I thought about the funeral
photos of GG Allin, whose brittle looks seemed to have been drawn
Pettibonesque onto his putty-like head, looks I think will never belong in
New York again, lying in repose the last American saint whose darkened
jockstrap, stained by profuse sweat, shined a light into a life indifferent to
the death that it knew would follow it, living forever in gin-tinged waves
the same black-and-white of the photographs that documented him
onstage. He would destroy this car, I thought, do whatever he could to
wreck it: piss on the Italian leather seats, smash the windows, rip the
steering wheel out and hurl it through the front window of the Le Pain
Quotidien nearby. I wish I could have picked Allin up and placed him in
the Porsche. In the few photographs of his dead body, he's mostly
unclothed. His head is slumped forward with his eyes reduced to
awkward, forced slits. In these images, he is too clean, brushed up to look
more substantial than his rushed, sketched-in presence must have been
in person. The images betray him. Reveler in blood and shit, piss and
cum, he might release it all into the Porsche, instruct us to fuck it up.
Liberate yourself by hurling excrement at what ought to be covered in
shit anyway. Punch the dashboard until it cracks, throw whatever is in
the glove box out the passenger-side window. Tear out the rearview
mirror. Smash the satellite radio. Pull the seat forward and start the
engine. Wreck it into what comes next.

WARM LEATHERETTE

1

LIL WAYNE RUINED DEATH.

In spring 2013, the rapper near fatally overdosed on sizzurp, an hallu-
cinogenic mixture of fruit soda and cough syrup, fortified with codeine
and promethazine. He seized up onstage and shook in his leopard-print
tights till almost electric departure from stage and world, was rushed
to the hospital and emerged alive, but not before nearly disappearing
forever into a fizzy, pharmaceutical afterlife.

Lil Wayne's "Love Me" describes women as agents of disappearance. The song not only privileges the male subject position in the various strata of intercourse, it valorizes the female as the necessary yet problematic participant that disrupts sex by her intervening consciousness. The female is an amnesiac object and the silent, organizing principle that enables Lil Wayne to proceed in the bliss of unthinking until he comes and forcibly "comes to his senses," at which point he abstracts the woman into the multitude of frictional figures who oppose him. His bitches who love him obliterate his need to maintain absence of responsibility with regard to the milieu of differing relationships that constitute his socio-sexual life. It's only when they actively engage that he returns to himself, to everything, wasted on sizzurp in the AM.

WOMEN RUINED THE RETURN.

In summer 2008, two NYPD officers accompanied an intoxicated East Village woman as she made her way home from a local bar. They entered her apartment with her, left, and returned several times throughout the night to rape her while she was barely conscious. She sued the NYPD, but the court found neither the surveillance tapes, which showed the police officers entering and leaving her home multiple times, nor her testimony sufficient cause to convict the two men of rape. The NYPD nevertheless dismissed the cops in an effort to placate the mounting tensions between it and the public it "serves and protects." Shortly thereafter, the two police officers left the city, the woman disappeared from the media that followed her, and I was detained in Fort Greene after I asked the police officer who had stopped me for an open container violation why he wasn't in the East Village raping women.

PRESSURE RUINED PROCEDURE.

Ten years after 9/11, the NYPD conducted numerous illegal operations against the occupiers camped near the site of the World Trade Center. I think you might remember this time, when we stood together in general assembly for hours and, later, waited for free pizza. What was, at first, a simple act of communalization became the far more mysterious idea, lurking around us, of the possible futures shooting up from the ground everywhere to form or demolish prisons, depending on your perspective. The NYPD dragged the protesters from their tents and into a mild winter. During the next year, the courts dropped the charges against many of the students, teachers, union workers, unsheltered people, and other activists after they became overburdened by the numerous legally-questionable cases. In those days, it was "fuck the police" and nothing else.

THE OVERBURDENED RUINED SYSTEM.

The poet Joan Retallack's poem "A I D / I / S A P P E A R A N C E" makes language disappear in a procedure that virally decomposes the found jargon of scientific inquiry, mimicking the fracturing of the body's defensive mechanisms by the AIDS virus. One time, I had tea with a friend my age living with HIV, and he told me he was struggling, over tea he was looking at me while a fire engine got stuck in traffic next to us and he said, though I could hardly hear him, he was struggling with. Rivulets of clouds formed in the sky above us. It is never summer anymore, it is only the eroded time of atypical weather. I was sitting in the café, reading a poem by Joan Retallack while Lil Wayne's "Love Me" played so loudly in someone else's headphones that I could hear the song several tables away. I thought (forgetting what my friend was struggling with), this song sums up some degraded feeling of the promoted self, jet set and breeze in the mix of medicinal waste, all to get the fuck back, as another poet, Lawrence Giffin, once put it, into that burning (private) plane.

MY PRIVATE PLANE RUINED JARGON.

In an extract of a paper on Retallack's poem, the academic Bryan Walpert, whose work I don't know, writes, "Retallack uses two connected lines of the postmodern critique of science—linguistic slippage and paradigm-dependency— not to subvert or to critique science as an end in itself but to return,"

summer in spring

winter in fall

spring in winter

fall in summer,

"but to return,"

spring in summer

fall in winter

winter in spring

summer in fall

"but to return attention to the human subject, specifically in the context of AIDS,"

fall in winter

spring in summer

summer in fall

winter in spring

"but to return" to the plane that had been set on fire by Lil Wayne's retinue of sociopaths (a celebrity is someone who desires to tell a joke that ends in the death of the entire world external to himself/herself) after they poured sizzurp all over the aisle seats and dropped matches onto the soaked leather.

2

You could say that by this point the night was in an advanced state of decomposition, illuminated by the flaming jet the local fire department could not put out. We stood by the runway, near the tall security fence, and drank Four Loko in the cool breeze.

SOMEONE RUINED ANONYMITY.

To return to my friend in summer, which was a kind of spring, he was telling me he was struggling with paying his bills while remaining an artist. What's become a cliché reverts to a very powerful reality when it's married to economics. We both have no money and as long as we've known each other (almost ten years) that has been the case. When we first met he was addicted to crystal meth and loved volcanoes. He liked to text me quotes from his favorite songs, sending the lines over and over again: "Hear the crushing wheel / Feel the steering wheel"; "You are my Ducati"; "I love the way you lie." He struck me as a thoroughly original person who would go much "further in life" than me, into and scaled by whatever indices of success, progress, and attention art could offer him in ten years. He's still addicted to crystal meth but has gotten over the volcanoes. In following his interest, I learned that volcanoes have a paradoxical effect on their environments, temporarily deadening life and disrupting fragile underwater ecosystems after they erupt. Later, these affected areas often become hotbeds of life, islands in the sea, and return with more force than before.

VOLCANOES RUINED SEASONS.

In 1816, the eruption of Mount Tambora eliminated that year's summer, resulting in very cold temperatures for June, July, and August; reduced crop yields; increased sickness; and general malaise. In July 1816, "incessant rainfall" during that "wet, ungenial summer" forced Mary Shelley, John William Polidori, Lord Byron, and Percy Shelley to stay indoors for much of their Swiss holiday. They decided to have a contest to see who could write the best horror story, leading Shelley to write *Frankenstein*, or *The Modern Prometheus* and Lord Byron to write "A Fragment," which Polidori later rewrote as *The Vampyre*—a precursor to Bram Stoker's *Dracula*. Byron was also inspired to write a poem, "Darkness," at the same time. Those days were like a magic show, each manipulating out of their occupants curious events in literature that created entirely new acts of expression via the arrival and dismissal of certain ideas they harbored about one another. Dracula ruined horror, but not before betraying his first author by finding another.

3

DEATH RUINED THE RETURN.

According to Wikipedia, the last member of any species is called an
endling. The entry names five individuals who occupied this final slot in
their respective evolutionary chains: Martha (Passenger Pigeon), Incas
(Carolina parakeet), Booming Ben (Heath hen), Benjamin (Tasmanian
tiger), Celia (Pyrenean ibex), Lonesome George (Pinta Island tortoise).
Recently, I've started to say their names to myself before I go to bed,
chanting and rechanting them like a nursery rhyme: Martha Incas /
Booming Ben / Lone-some George / Cel-i-a and Ben-ja-min.

ENDLINGS RUINED DEATH.

Tim writes to me to say that an endling triumphs over extinction because it is literally the death of the death of its species. When they disappear or are stuffed and mounted in the Smithsonian in Washington, D.C., they take with them the demise of everyone who might have survived them. I love these endlings and hope that love, within its power, can restore them to life. Or it is love, I think, that allows the future to finally emerge out of linear time in order to bring us back to the starting point. Or love is an engine that reroutes the disappeared and returns them to their rightful place in the hierarchy of things we've lost but which will soon reappear in the present more alive than they were before. Or.

Repeat yourself a few times, say goodbye, listen to Selena Gomez, look at Tumblr, take a shower, read the news, play "Love Me," say goodbye, love me.

Repeat yourself a few times, read Dennis Cooper, text a friend, go home, say goodbye, drink coffee, buy a chair, listen to Selena Gomez, look at Tumblr, say goodbye, go to bed, wake up in the middle of the night, say goodbye, listen to Selena Gomez, look at Wikipedia, read the endlings, say goodbye, love me.

SELENA GOMEZ RUINED LIL WAYNE.

Selena Gomez's "Naturally" is a counterpoint to Lil Wayne's "Love Me" in its radical affirmation of the other as an animating agent within the self and suggests a status update in terms of the relationship between her and the subject of love. I stand on the roof of my apartment on Park Place and Nostrand Avenue, looking at Crown Heights in early spring, waiting for the rain promised by my weather app, listening to her unravel the logic of pure, scattering desire as she channels the voice of another, a voice which she internalizes to express in her own stunning hit the maximizing effect of listening to someone you love speak, a lover we do not hear, but who invigorates us, too. "How you choose to express yourself, it's all your own, I can tell it comes naturally." The act of speaking as one would "naturally" speak takes her breath away, supernaturalizing her romance into the compatible forces of thunder and lightning. She is nature. Pink sheets, fluttering skies, summer noon, drawn shades, lava lamp, flaming jet, purple light, server crash, shadowed face, smudged dark, my home, your islands, Martha, Incas, sure thing, August palette, hands held, lips, lipgloss, Benjamin, new job, smoking weed, Lonesome George, as it was, Booming Ben, yes of course, Crown Heights, Celia, flash drive, sleep well, cab ride, good night, forever forever, forever certain, it comes naturally.

TRACK STAR

all day I dream about
my Adidas tracksuit

*

I wrote this fragment in my notebook a few weeks after I had fallen in
love with the tracksuit. My obsession began when a friend wore an
Adidas jacket and black pants one night to drinks at a bar. In the dark,
I misread his outfit as a full tracksuit—a surprise choice for what I had
(wrongly) thought of as a date. Later, when I told him that I thought he
looked good in athletic wear, he said he wasn't wearing a full tracksuit,
just the jacket. Still, I really thought he looked hot in his imaginary
tracksuit and after that night I often fantasized about boys wearing
the semi-form-fitting synthetic fabric—in bedrooms and soccer fields,
subways and dive bars. The tracksuit defines enough of the body to
describe its shape but not enough to reveal the higher definition of
its contours. The tracksuit, like the plastic it's made from, works for

different people in different ways, and this difference diversifies its social use. The tracksuit evokes the English, English skinheads but also the London riots of 2011, when thousands of impoverished Londoners exploited by shitty economics and ignored by the stewards of that decaying system took to the streets to smash windows, overturn cars, and set houses on fire. In the YouTube videos of these riots, many of the men are wearing tracksuits. The tracksuit evokes soccer players at the World Cup. It evokes NYU students who are too lazy to wear normal clothing when they walk down University Place to their ugly library on Washington Square South. Russian men can be seen wearing them while they beat up gay rights activists, who themselves are wearing tracksuits. The tracksuit is ageless and fits anyone for any moment. In this regard, the tracksuit is an image for an emancipatory politics that might emerge from the ecological wreckage of our moment as a flexible, evasive, even nonspecific opposition to the current economic configuration of "the world." One size, more or less, fits all. Also, not. It's a certain gay look I currently like. My friend really did look hot when I thought he was wearing a tracksuit. The tracksuit is versatile: its synthetic fabric is optimized for comfort and durability, meaning it can withstand varying weather conditions and climates. Wearing my own Adidas tracksuit and jogging through Central Park in the fall, beneath the changing leaves, I think about the autumnal blur canopied over me that I never really stop to parse. Leaves change via a complicated process I look up and can say happens because of the presence of chlorophyll in the leaves, a pigment held in an organelle called a chloroplast. When chlorophyll is abundant in the leaf's cells, as it is during the growing season, its green color dominates and masks the colors of any other pigments that may be present. As daylight decreases and the days and nights cool, the veins that carry fluids into and out of the leaf are gradually closed off as a layer of special cork cells forms at the stem. As this cork layer develops, water and mineral intake into the leaf is reduced, slowly at first, and then more rapidly. It is during this time that the chlorophyll begins to decrease and the color begins to change. The leaf slowly lowers its green mask. I circle Central Park as the light shifts back and the evening takes on the sharp, clear air that carries the city light toward me, swamping the trees with the bright, urban night. I finish my run and stop at the edge of the park, near 59th Street and Broadway. A man selling pretzels and wearing a tracksuit looks at me and shouts, "You need water?"

1. PVG to SFO, Shanghaied to Old Gold Mountain; youtube tutorial, how to dye your faded bluejean sunsets to black (3 sages grimace/ smile at the industrial dust cloud banding across the Pacific, radio-active isotopes of the visual-virtual's uncontrollable fission). Amazing that Americans can obtain so much mass, approximate stuff of two or three people in Beijing. Meanwhile political prisoners have been harvested for organs, transhipment via former soviet republics into wealthy diabetics and career alcoholics: because nickelodeon's green goo is people, appropriated lyrics of mourning (napalm girl, coal miner's daughter).

2. The fortune-cookie reads: "—Never mistake a killer for a koan." Language lesson on the back: "Sociopathic: without any empathy. SEE: Henry Miller as a boy, deliberately farting at the funerary casket of

another child, to express his contempt for both friendship and sorrow; SEE ALSO, Marquis de Sade, violently abusing a prostitute. Note: Critics tend to confuse sociopathy with a purported,"—absolute freedom of artistic/spiritual vision," because they themselves fear empathy as the taint of influence and/or restricted, unreflective thinking. Above all else, the critic desires to appear sophisticated, savvy, and in on the joke. The pure sociopath desires to tell a joke that ends in the death of the entire world external to himself/herself. Lucky lottery numbers: "Un Coup de Dés / enfants ont cassé les carreaux." ((Justine Redwood Bieber exclaims as (s/he) falls: "—for nowadays the world is lit by lightning. Blow out your candles, California, and so say goodbye … "))

3. Marionette carved from the salvaged timber of Hollywood patios and trellises, from memories of Del Monte, from disco ember's cocaine glow, from shredded *Archie* comics and fat Elvis funk fantasies: Terius Youngdell Nash knows how to string out an American dream, soul-sadness submerged, but never auto-tuned past auto-wreck, ignition. Rockets rolling somewhere over gravity's rainbow, because music becomes our only memory when we can't look back at Mississippi John Hurt's home in the Delta blues as we contrail above Embarcadero. Whereas Max Martin's genius is pure pop explosion, here today and gone tomorrow like a coalition of the willing. Funny enough, this entire passage might have been cribbed from a Pitchfork music review, in the guise of a grim-faced hipster homage to American Gothic: stick it to 'em, etc etc etc. (("—For all flesh is as grass, and all the glory of man as the flower of grass. The grass withereth, and the flower thereof falleth away … / "—Or I guess the grass is itself a child …))

4. Joke written on the back of an airplane napkin: "—The oldest man with a Bieber tattoo is named Catullus #63, the parable of Attis and Cybele." Neither smile nor grimace: partial facial paralysis, singing to himself as he looks out the window. The fellow seated next to him's

engrossed in an episode of *Saved By the Bell*. The tattoo above his own heart reads: Buddy Holly.

— posted 04/08/2013 at 19:50 by >

MONICA MAJOLI

I am at the Frieze Art Fair

on May 18, 2013, and it's

raining on the inflatable

Paul McCarthy sculpture

of Jeff Koons's balloon dog.

I'm looking at a painting

by Monica Majoli,

at complex forms rendered

shadow in the geometry

of available flesh,

dissolution of youth in the dark,

this opening in me like a wound

without recourse to a mend

is totally Frieze.

Frieze is like those jobs

that say you'll be compensated

commensurate with experience.

How many times have I read that

as "commiserate," thinking

we might "weigh in"

together to express sympathy

for my having to beg you

to pay me a living wage, itself a term

so vexed in its little assertion

of a metaphysics of cash

it hurls me further

into whatever anally tiny

rabbit hole I've already found myself

crawling down, toward

a demon rabbit with a Koch brother's face.

The number of times reverses me

into ecstasies, crucified on the cross

of precarious employment

but in so less royally

a martyrdom I am rent

anonymous by it.

Frieze is kind of like that,

except it's about buying art,

which I can't do.

And writing about it

is much worse,

so I've been reading

Bruce Hainley to get away

from "the process" of doing so.

Bruce is the LA-based art critic

and poet who writes

about artists that a lot of us

don't pay much attention to,

like Lee Lozano. She

was so pissed off

at the art world

she threw it away,

left New York after a dispute

over her rent with her landlord

in a final piece called *Dropout*.

She more or less spent the rest of her life

living a single, continuous performance

as someone totally outside

of the art world, reclaiming

the space that surrounds it,

redoubled in sequestration

of the suburbs where how many of us originate,

her the suburbs of Texas, me

the suburbs of Florida, Monica Majoli

the generalized suburb of Los Angeles.

I'm reading Bruce's writing in *Pep Talk*,

a small art mag produced somewhere,

I can't tell where from its website,

but probably LA,

where everything cool

comes from to die back east.

Ben Fama lent it to me

one afternoon after I quoted this from a blogpost of Bruce's in an
email to him: "I like pros, especially when it comes to tennis and rent
boys"—and here I'm really wondering if the pun on prose consolidates
Bruce's feeling toward it versus poetry under the sign of sex, which
Bruce sometimes pays for, in order to direct us toward the pleasure
of its use-function when monetized, a pleasure seldom associated
with poetry, and one that might lead to the company of more pros. He
continues: "If I can get a twofer, and the trick looks like Rafael Nadal, I'm
in heaven."

I'm in heaven

when I google image search Rafael Nadal

and find him radiating solar joy

on the home page of the *New York Times*,

having just advanced in some open

I've already forgotten the name of,

proving to us

that the champions

of the world

still wear jockey shorts.

I might collapse in a heap

he's so hot. Bruce

has been everywhere

in my life recently. Last night,

I went to a party

and ran into Alan Gilbert.

We discussed Bruce's

really great new piece

on Monica Majoli in *Artforum*.

Bruce starts with this description

of Michael Jackson, whose death

spiked such an inarticulate

slush of feeling,

of feeling so sick to my

stomach when a friend

called me to tell me the news

while I was walking down Magazine Street

in New Orleans,

I almost threw up

and had to sit down. Bruce writes: "Forgoing outright atrocity, of which there is so much—too much—right now, aren't the 'life,' 'body,' and 'face' of Michael Jackson in the running for some of the most abstract events of the last century? (I use the tweezers of scare quotes to approach each of those precarious terms because I'm not certain I could handle them at all otherwise.) 'His' face and its occlusion, in the final years, when any nose he had was entirely prosthetic (not to mention the permanent eyeliner and chemical bleaching), became a brutal inversion of all the solar joy he beamed as a young performer—that is, when his face appeared at all, since he was prone to wearing what appeared to be a niqab, 'transgendering' his complicated presence as much as cloaking it. I'm bringing up Jackson's 'desire,' every bit as abstract as it was intractable, because his 'desire' strikes me as even more elusive and imponderable, although many during his lifetime supposed they understood what he repressed or compensated for, even if a fundamental component of whatever his desire might have been remained the sense that he seemed constitutionally uncoupled (and uncouplable)." Wow, right?

Monica's work is really great.

In particular this crucifixion-like

scene of a BDSM orgy

in which one subject

is hung up on a cross of boys

who pleasure him:

one boy is half burying

his face in Christ's ass

while another boy has the tip

of Christ's cock dipped in his mouth.

I guess I like Monica's painting

for the ecstasy in which Christ finds himself

nailed to a cross by bodies who crave him,

subjugating fear, this physical imposition

of desire that restrains him

and through which he finds himself

desirable. S/M frees you

to a sex without romance,

formats desire on these

interpersonal axes that belie

the fantasy that drives it,

allowing our interactions

to match a preset system

of behaviors we are already aware of

and introducing within its grid

a notational set of inputs

that activate certain desired

outputs. Nothing is veiled

in order to forefront

the point of the act

in the first place,

and from this the world's

primal motion is set onward—

So, like, I know I like

to get tied down

and jerked off. And for my partner,

that's really, really clear,

you know? Frieze

is kind of like that, too,

totally honest

about its tradeshow quality,

even if that honesty betrays an unhappiness

not quite depressed in its paralyzed tears

but certainly deprived of recourse

to the promissory world of liberation

it might have once suggested.

Flow my tears, the painter said. Or, as Majoli once wrote, "I only paint actual experiences, not fantasies. Within that I elaborate and alter things in the environment, but the activities and the rooms and objects in the interiors are 'factual.' So in this way I view the paintings as documentary, as a way for me to memorialize events and relationships. The male sex scenes began when a close friend of mine started to go to underground pissparties and became increasingly involved with S/M sex. I had always been fascinated by his anonymous encounters with men. I envied the nonverbal quality and the absolute sexual abandon of his experiences. AIDS confused all this—and I began to wonder about this decision to pursue this despite the consequences. I understood his desire to 'connect' through sex regardless of the cost. I viewed these paintings as religious, although I still can't explain this. As I continued to paint I slowly realized that I was identifying, uncomfortably so, with the masochist in the composition. I switched reluctantly to images of myself when I fell deeply in love with a woman and felt compelled to paint her after our relationship ended. These autobiographical paintings all involve dildos. Right now, I'm working on a round painting in which I'm fucking myself with one dildo while sucking on a double-headed dildo. The feeling I want to express is of a huge emptiness and isolation. I haven't figured out why dildos are the central 'props' in those paintings. I think it has to do with this false tool—that the mind wants to make real. Using a fake device to try to communicate with a lover or comfort oneself—so in a way this communication or connection is ultimately doomed. The body fragments are self-portraits that I began when I first painted the scenes. In this way I felt it was like a conversation between the intimacy of the details and the voyeuristic, removed quality of the scenes. I feel that both bodies of work concern the same issues—the body fragments address mortality and vulnerability more directly. I chose parts of the body that seemed particularly fragile. The parts are either cut or in a state of exposure to describe the perils of love and simultaneously, the compulsion to love."

I'm sitting in a café

in Brooklyn, texting James La Marre,

listening to Ariel Pink's

"Symphony of a Nymph,"

writing about Monica Majoli.

It's late spring,

surprisingly brisk

for this rainy mid-May. I guess

I'm so over "it,"

another season's change

so vexed as to render

its character meaningless

in its punishing irregularity,

over even the famous path of trees

that line Eastern Parkway,

where I sat texting this morning

below the lush panoply

of sky slinking

over the concrete.

I texted Ben,

I texted Kate,

I called my mom,

and yet the simplicity of these actions

failed to regulate my sense

of their eventual removal

from the things I do. Looking back,

doesn't everything seem cryptic,

sealed in its place

a symbol of the near impossible exchange

between times once alike but denied

the way back to one another,

like the scrunched face of Rafael Nadal

when he lost Wimbledon,

his face no longer legible as a holy thing,

I thought wow, Rafael,

if I could be there for you, I would.

Anyway, wherever I am

I'm not with you,

whoever you in the plural are,

by now I'm all the way down the line

into garbage time,

embalmed in its vision

of an apocalypse

tearing up what's left of

life in universe zero,

where perhaps our love

will be stored

on a hard drive

forever, fastened

to its post-physical life away

from things as they really are.

Maybe it's the afterglow of the end

in Monica Majoli's paintings,

a light which dissolves us

in one form only to restructure us

in another. Who is my preserver?

Descended into this

crystal hard drive,

I am stationed among the nodes

asserting me in the various networks

that have become *feeling*.

Soon the one world

we have found flattened

in its emergent disunity

will annihilate itself

in a compromise with fate

and the physics

of this cooling universe

dissipating so slowly

it will be like nothing

ever changed.

I WENT DOWN TO THE BEACH

I went down to the beach and wrote a book called *The Beach*, inspired by *Heart of Darkness*, a novel about the perils of inadequately supervised interaction between codified behavior and the Other. To put it more directly, I wrote a novel based on a novel about the degradation of white leadership in the face of non-Western local practice exoticized in fantasy rather than observation. Exterior: the jungle. Interior: Dark night of the white man's soul. In my novel about the beach, which takes place in a remote region of Thailand, a boy is given a map by a man named Daffy Duck that points to a beach where few people have ever been, largely because of how treacherous the path to it is. Richard, the main character, leads a French couple and later two Harvard graduates on an adventure to the beach, an adventure in which they encounter frictional social elements (like an evil marijuana plantation) that attempt to deter them from traveling to the beach. Finally, they jump off a waterfall, float down a river, and meet a highly organized totalitarian society of expatriates ruled by an American woman named Sal. This is the most significant reference to *Heart of Darkness*. Their time at the beach is filled with curious events that create a compelling plot of intrigue, like when they run out of rice and Jed, "the enigmatic loner of the group," volunteers to go for a rice run. Richard, accompanying him, realizes it is time to escape. Tribe members die. Social complexities contribute to pain, paranoia, and euthanasia. I would describe all of this in greater detail but you have to read my book *The Beach*. To escape, Richard spikes the tribe's stew one night with marijuana so that everyone is incapacitated by an "overloaded high." He flees with the French couple and Jed, into the night, "back to civilization."

I went down to the beach and adapted my book called *The Beach* for the big screen, inspired by *Apocalypse Now*, a movie about the perils of inadequately supervised interaction between codified behavior (played by Marlon Brando) and the Other (played by a number of underpaid local Filipino workers). To put it more directly, I adapted my novel using a film about the degradation of white leadership in the face of non-Western local practice exoticized in fantasy rather than observation. Exterior: the jungle. Interior: Dark night of Marlon Brando's soul. In the film version of my novel about the beach, which takes place in a remote region of Thailand, a boy (played by Leonardo DiCaprio) is given a map by a man named Daffy Duck (played by Robert Carlyle) that points to a beach where few people have ever been, largely because of how treacherous the path to it is. Richard, the main character, leads a French couple (played by Virginie Ledoyen and Guillaume Canet) and later two American surfers on an adventure to the beach, an adventure in which they encounter frictional social elements (like an evil marijuana plantation) that attempt to deter them from traveling to the beach. Finally, they jump off a waterfall, float down a river, and meet a highly organized totalitarian society of expatriates ruled by an American woman named Sal (played by Tilda Swinton). This is the most significant reference to *Apocalypse Now*. Their time at the beach is filled with curious events that create a compelling plot of intrigue, like when Christo (played by Staffan Kihlbom) is injured and Sal volunteers to go to the mainland for medical supplies. Richard realizes it is time to escape. Tribe members die. Social complexities contribute to pain, paranoia, and euthanasia. I would describe all of this in greater detail but you have to see my movie *The Beach*. To escape, Richard flees the tribe after the marijuana farmers violently disrupt the community's activities. He flees with Sal, into the night, "back to civilization."

At the premier of *The Beach*, Leonardo DiCaprio stole away from the theater three times to the use the restroom. Sitting near him, I couldn't help but notice him leaving so often, and decided after the third time he exited the theater to follow him to see if anything was wrong. Didn't he like the film I'd adapted from the book I'd written? I pushed my way out of my row.

As I walked up the theater aisle, past friends glittering in the changing light of the projection, each smiling or nodding at me as they watched me pass by, I thought about the conditions under which I'd begun the novel. I had originally meant to set *The Beach* in New York in 2012. It was going to be about the hostilities of an emergent, troubling climate in which a flurry of deadly natural events wreck the lives of those living in the city. Shortly after Hurricane Sandy "compromised" the coast and shut down much of New Jersey, Staten Island, Brooklyn, and Manhattan, the news wrote my novel itself and I decided that I would invert the reality into a narrative of departure rather than arrival. I wanted to chase the storm, so I set my novel and my film at the beach, away from a city broken by the weather that would play no role in my work.

I entered the lobby and asked an attendant if he knew where Leo had gone. "He's in the bathroom to the right," he said. "He didn't look well, actually. I think he's planning to go."

"Thanks," I said. In the hallway that led to the bathroom, the theater piped in Katy Perry's "Firework." Its poppy burst of good feelings and helium-inflated enthusiasm for the body unleashed in a rush of heady endorphins, acceptance of anyone and everyone no matter who or what they are, felt incongruous outside my brittle, unsettling film, in the silent lobby with its dim lights that made even my most beautiful, famous friends look like strange ghosts, haunting the image of themselves. I pictured Katy throwing her arms open to Budapest in the music video, fireworks exploding from her breasts into the hot night and wished at the moment I was there with her, in Hungarian summer and not in New York's brutal winter.

In the bathroom, I found Leo sobbing on the white tile floor. I rushed over to him.

"Are you OK?" I asked. He shook his head. "What's wrong?"

"I'm not exactly sure, I guess ... I just ... it's that I'm so rarely bothered by my own work, like upset by it. But for some particular reason *The Beach* feels different, almost like it's this narrative for a career I don't really want, from androgynous objet d'art to streetwise tough guy, a little fucked up by the world, yah, but still a real strong guy, if that makes any sense. Like do I want that? It gets under my skin with an energy that makes me feel so fucking strange."

"That *is* strange," I said. "I hadn't meant it that way."

"I know," he said and began to cry again.

I held Leo for a few minutes before I asked him if he wanted me to call his driver. His red and tearstained face lit with real gratitude. "Could you?" he said. "I need to go home."

I pulled out my cell and called his driver. I pulled Leo up and helped him out of the bathroom and into the lobby, where we waited for his driver. Tilda emerged from the theater and rushed over to us.

"Is everything all right?" Tilda asked.

"Everything is all right," I said. "Leo isn't feeling well, so I'm sending him home."

The driver appeared in the lobby and Leo went to him. Tilda and I followed them outside, to the corner of the street and the avenue where the driver double-parked the car.

We watched Leo get into the limo, waved goodbye, then returned to *The Beach*, just as, on screen, our star jumped off the waterfall, into the river that would take him to Tilda.

In *Apocalypse Now*, US special operations officers reverse the geographical trajectory of *The Beach* by going away from it, into the jungle, where they meet the tribe where Kurtz has installed himself as an unflinching, totalitarian leader. In a moment of extra-literary affinity, Brando quotes T. S. Eliot's "The Hollow Men," which has an epigraph from *Heart of Darkness*. On a micro-level, the US special operations officers are tasked with the same objective as that of the greater US military in Vietnam: intervention in an emergent political order so that its potentially harmful aspects are neutralized and non-Communist leadership is restored. Despite their small number relative to Kurtz's slaves, they succeed; however, in killing the American and setting the Vietnamese free, they pre-stage the eventual failure of the American invasion of Vietnam, the Vietcong's defeat of the imperialist overlord and its acid-bombing campaigns across the landscape. *The Beach* defuses the imbalances of competitive polities, entraps the unraveling plot to reincorporate disambiguated bodies into a tribe of limitless potential. Great spray of light across Thailand. The beaches were untouched before my film crew arrived; we destroyed the landscape to create paradise. The dunes were removed as were many of the palm trees in order to create the site of bliss in the audience's mind. I saw the film, I went down to the beach, I removed my shoes. A little crab walked in front of me. I watched as it scuttled by slowly until it buried itself in the sand.

Once, when I was writing my novel, I went into one of the very last dive bars in lower Manhattan and met a veteran from the Gulf War.

It was after Halloween, the hurricane had passed, and the power had been restored to the city. I sat at the bar drinking a whiskey on the rocks when he approached me from behind and asked if I wanted to have sex with him in the bathroom. He had a massive, muscular figure shaped like an inverted pyramid. He wore fatigues and was covered in tattoos so worn down by exposure to the sun that they looked like Rorschach blots on his skin.

Swaying, he slung his arm around me and said, "You'd have fun." I told him no and asked where he was from. "Virginia. But I was stationed here after Iraq and I've never left." We talked about the war, and I wondered if he had been responsible for the deaths of children. "If you won't sleep with me," he said, "I'm going to just go jerk off in the toilet. Do you want to join me?" he said. "I'll be in the toilet."

I watched him disappear into the back. Thirty minutes later he was found soaked in his own urine, passed out between the toilet and the wall. The bouncer dragged him out into the street while the bartender called the police.

Leonardo DiCaprio directed his driver to take him to beach. When they arrived at Far Rockaway, he asked him to wait while he went down to the water to think. The sky was the color of steel, the mottled gray of New York in winter, generalized and monolithically opposite the lightness of coming spring, when Leo would finally be at play. The dunes had been mostly destroyed by Sandy, replaced by Christmas trees lying in neat rows along the coastline. The branches caught the sand flying up from the water toward the streets and homes. Eventually they would be covered up, restoring the dunes to how they once were. Leo took his headphones out and stuffed them into his coat pockets. He walked down to the waterline and looked at the ocean. It felt like nothing, only the huge swelling of the absence of things, present for him but at the same time annihilating—a vector in a dream he slides down into oblivion. Damage is unplanned obsolescence that contradicts the order of things. Katy Perry in Budapest, Leo at the beach. Damage is a reminder that glamour is contingent on its destructibility. He placed his hands in his coat pockets and thought about what to do next, whether he would return to the theater or fly home, back to Los Angeles. Despite how cold it was, he felt warm, and the moment of seeing a piece of cardboard fly into the sea generated in him the weird desire to say to the accumulating waves, "I haven't told you of the most beautiful things in my lives, watching the ripple of their loss disappear along the shore, underneath ferns, face downward in the ferns my body, the naked host to my many selves, shot by a guerilla warrior or dumped from a car into ferns which are themselves *journalières*. The hero, trying to unhitch his parachute, stumbles over me. It is our last embrace. I have forgotten my loves, and chiefly that one, the cancerous statue, which my body could no longer contain, and against my will, against my love, become art. I could not change it into history and so remember it. I have lost what is always and everywhere present, the scene of my selves, the occasion of these ruses, which I myself and singly now must kill to save the serpent in their midst."

YOU ARE MY DUCATI

Between the wars, Antonio Ducati and sons founded Società Scientifica
Radio Brevetti Ducati in Bologna to produce radio parts. Repeatedly
bombed and later reformed as a manufacturer of motorized bicycles
after the defeat of the Axis, Ducati is recalled by R&B artist Ciara sixty
years later in a one piece wrapped in fur, "You are my Ducati," a mo-
torcycle more theory than vehicle, you whom I ride are my everything.
Also, Ciara of *Fantasy Ride*, the never-too-real always glistening at the
edge of the sparkly ethos of forward motion she calls "love sex mag-
ic," what she says she'll "drive her body around." Middling production
of second-rate bikes for a time, yet eventually love sex magic seized
in the automatic transmission, the desmodromic valve. Ducati finally
distinguished itself by means of speed with the Mach 1, a motorcycle
that could travel at 100 mph (its lightweight frame the color of the bill
of Ciara's Atlanta Braves baseball cap), exceptional in its design, now
a collector's item. (It doesn't ride.) List of objects that appear in the
video for Ciara's "Ride": a car, a mechanical bull, a chair. The Ducati
Multistrada 1200, a bike of such sophistication that it rides like a breeze

out of some future world, doesn't appear in the *Ride* video, but its presence directs the trajectories of these objects in their collision with Ciara: "All up on your frame, baby say my name." Everything around her rises to gossipy transcendence. Ducati's founding mission was to manufacture the radio, a point now echoed in Ciara's music of objective romance, constitutive in its mysteries, but perhaps only a kind of body glue, like that which secures the one-piece.

Since first listening to Ciara's "Ride," her 2010 chart-topper about the reversal of expectation, gender trouble loosened in the declaration that her man is her Ducati, the mobilizing object parked in the garage that begs you, slick with rain, to take him for a spin, I've become obsessed with the Italian motorcycle company, specifically their Multistrada 1200. Ciara repurposes the bike as an interpretative tool: You are my Ducati, she sings, converting the male body of her rapidly shifting attention into the mobilizing figure of European racing sports. Where does Ciara want to go? Most likely she wants to leave you behind, lonely in the sunset as she flees with luxury trailing behind her. Her perfectly mani-cured fingers grip the handlebars. You are my Ducati, utilizing the rhet-oric of sex to mechanize her partner into the process of love as engine of speed, you make me want to ride, glassy body exteriorized into a system of gears hieroglyphic in their trippy gorgeousness, building into a complex of metaphors a second life more exhilarating in its imitation of how well, and fast, she dances, than the first—even at the risk that it might circle back to collide with you. The song has really become rather important to me.

     Ludacris, in his interlude toward the end of "Ride," tries his best to retrieve Ciara from her liberating theory by integrating her into a series of confusing sports metaphors that situate the male in the consummate exclusionary field where he might feel most at ease, soft wet grass under the stadium lights: the football game—hurrahed by cheerleaders, the only women on the field. Their presence in the game doesn't interrupt the play of male athletes, it cheers on the spectacle of their bodies beneath heavy equipment. In football, Ludacris can finally assert himself by forcibly removing Ciara: "I put her out like a light … Call me the Terminator … I gotta put her to bed." Sports, for Ludacris, reestablishes his active, rather than passive, mobility, patching his name onto Drew Brees's in order to "score" with a woman. He tries to capture the energy that would exempt him from becoming a Ducati, supercharging the song with his own flittering agency in the third-person: "I throw it in / touch down / he scores." But together, Ciara and Ludacris are totally out of sync—"you better cc me," he sings, to which Ciara replies, ignoring his call for office etiquette in order to restore her own wish: "He love the way I ride it. He can't stand to look away." But where else might a Ducati look?

She mounts the bike—not quite the Multistrada 1200, not quite Ludacris, but rather a dreamy, pulsing confluence of object relations, a paralyzing network of competitive masculinities, each sinking under the weight of its indebtedness to a rule of social law—luxury epitomized in the exemplary technology of speed, derived from an upper-class music of leisure transported from Italy to New York—suddenly foiled in its power by its own controlling interests. She rides it.

When I listen to Ciara, I think about what it would be like to rent a Ducati and joyride up the West Side Highway, onto 9G, toward upstate at the start of fall. I think about how fast I could go—and at what point up ahead I might permanently lock myself into the moment between ride and accident, the twin poles I imagine a motorcyclist, weaving between cars on the narrow roads of the Catskills, pivots between with a glee that accelerates toward a death indistinguishable from life. As for me, I'm transfixed by the moment speed hits a wall and the totalizing event that both binds and unbinds us to it (what I want to drive my body around), an accident breathtaking in its approach, arrives at last to slow me way the fuck down. Ciara's dancing speeds up and slows down the known world in its claim on global time, New York's autumn

splashed against this life

measured out in miles

per hour, to say nothing

of its explication in gallons

of oil. To ride breezily against the backdrop

of huge cost, to endorse its rush as you

fall into it, to drop low like Ciara,

below the adoring skies

of the Hudson Valley

on a Multistrada 1200 the color

of Ludacris's sunglasses in the *Ride* video,

tempering agency via a touchdown

at the 2009 Super Bowl

yet smashed into the wall

of Ciara's poetics of speed

he is hurled toward,

incapable of seeing it

before him. Listening

to Ludacris, I feel flung at her, too,

like we're riding a Ducati into fall,

and, suddenly, we slam

into the season's shifting weather

and are released

into the beige, yellow, and red

of autumn, pastels that sunset over us, foundering in a haze at the
horizon veering from greenish blue to purple like money burning in
your hands.

Later, Ciara and I meet in a semidarkened vacant mall and
wander through various shops until we find a somewhat new JCPen-
ney, swept up in creamsicle light. When we enter the department store,

it turns out that Ciara and I are together the 10,000th customer and have won a Ducati motorcycle of our choice. It's a spectacular moment, one christened by confetti as Ciara leans over in her fur to accept the hand of the JCPenney employee who congratulates us. Muzak elaborates the celebratory atmosphere of the empty department store, where no one is celebrating, at the moment of our win. I blush as I realize that here I am, with Ciara, pop star unfixed to a music that would determine her, like really it's all pretty plastic in its one-size-fits-all quality, and though she's in love with her beau Future, she's in love with me, too. The JCPenney manager greets us and leads us to the back lot of the department store, into the cool breeze of a late October night, where there are ten bikes lined up, each glinting in the street light. Ciara selects the Multistrada 1200 and says, "This is the one."

"I love it," I tell her. The manager smiles and removes a contract from his suit pocket. He unfolds it and hands it to us. I don't spend any time reviewing the endless pages of terms and conditions and sign immediately. He hands over the keys and the deed to the Multistrada 1200.

Ciara mounts the bike, which, at that moment, doesn't *not* feel like me, and asks me to climb on. Where should we go? she asks. I can hardly speak. This moment becomes a second dream in which I imagine where I might go, out of here, so that even when I do shake myself out of it I can't let go. I remember seeing a Ducati two falls ago on Canal before joining my friends below a moment sparkling in the presence of the Goldman Sachs employees who toasted our protest

as the actualized politics

of community eroded

downtown's teary sense

of its ensconced

kingdom, like

we got it, OK,

you don't want this to end,

but we do, even though in a sense

the end brought about a separate

conflict anterior to its original:

how to continue

and still be friends. On Canal,

I spotted a man on a Ducati motorcycle,

perhaps a banker or some other agent

of wealth beyond reproach,

and thought of all gross injustices served

us this, the rich white guy on his bike,

was some reminder of the fault line

that might eventually open up

to swallow him down. If histories

go fast they go faster when compelled

toward an inevitable terminus

made finally realer

in the earnest wish for its sudden

arrival, this delicate

egg of relations I'd like to hurl

at a riot cop's helmet. The Ducati

looped in steel a black, cold ring

I would place on my own finger

but can't because I make

pretty much nothing

and can scarcely afford the rent

of my Crown Heights apartment

let alone a motorcycle for $15k. Ciara is right: we are each our own
Ducati, molded into the steel frame into which we can lean, one night
in fall, to ride you, all the bodies upon whom one rides, impaled by such

disasters as the sudden recognition that you can't stand to look away, caught in the remaining sunlight, and yet must.

The cop, egg dripping from the visor lowered over the helmet, runs forward with his club.

"Catch me in the mall, I can do this, however you want, I can do it up and down, I can do it in circles," Ciara sings, articulating a body I cannot call my own, but might locate somewhere close to it a secondary body in which he love the way I ride it, impounded by the desire to manipulate and be manipulated into the shape of others, to become with others yet another who might race back with a club of my own, the shape of the fastest motorcycle we can find. Sleek in the discourse that describes us as the inimitable technology designed to destroy one another, I love to ride it.

Outside the JCPenney, Ciara breaks my concentration and asks if I want to go. I hesitate to ask her where, knowing the location she might suggest would be essentially absent everywhere except where it televises itself semirandomly, against the bark of a tree in the woods upstate or in the champagne glass at evening or the broken visor of the egg-soaked cop, now falling back. You make me want to ride it, Ciara sings to Ludacris standing under the street light as he debates whether or not to mount the Ducati. At this, he atomizes into the moment his appearance is rendered nostalgic, a translucent memory that hardly registered at all yet for a time was all-controlling, an event that is replaced by another in a cycle of replacement too rapid to isolate the particulars of.

Actuated methods in a cluster of instruments, loss of the self in the attenuated seams of biopolitical production, blue-faced for the fallen world dropping even faster: Tell him I'm a gymnast, tell him I'm a Ducati, tell him to get off the street, tell him to ride, tell him to step back, tell him to find me later, tell him to check

his phone, tell him to replace

its cracked screen, tell him to take

the A train on Canal, tell him to cross

the bridge, tell him to hand over

his fucking money, tell him

to meet me in the mall,

tell him the history of ideas

is a series of miscalculations

each demarcating various

assumptions of mapped space,

reveries that mangle

then re-cohere into lesser,

but nevertheless raging

trajectories of departure. Tell him I want

to go faster, into the air, beyond

the accident of our moment,

the point where an invisible rope

yanked taut between

impassable hours of leisure

pulls back, a little harder,

the second you resist, and you fly

from the vehicle hurling you

forward. Speed

is a market of energy

directed toward excess.

Once you stop, then what?

We can't stop, yet the consuming fantasy

to do so upgrades my sense of the need

to go all the faster.

We move at some new rate

toward the indeterminate point

at which something happens

but simultaneously obscures

the character that would

enable us to define it—up

the mountain along

the mountain road into

a world caught in the midst

of its material ceremonies as they

break down. I see something

in them, probably the face of Ciara,

caught between the leaves,

annotating each glimpse

of the woods with another

opaque name heroizing

this yet unbranded age. I ride

into it, a future slashed

at the horizon, lying

just below the setting sun, into

the point at which

it rises over me to summer

in the shadows shifting

so rapidly

as to seem

to not exist

at all.

ACKNOWLEDGMENTS

I could not have written this book without the insight, advice, and friendship of Ben Fama, Ed Halter, Ian Hatcher, Lucy Ives, Kevin Killian, Trisha Low, Jacolby Satterwhite, Tim Terhaar, and Carl Williamson. Most of all, I am grateful for the attention and continuous support of Stephen Motika, who firmly believed in this book before it was ever a book. Some of these pieces first appeared in the *Boston Review, The Destroyer, Epiphany, Fence, The Miami Rail, Out of Order, Pocket Notes,* and *Triple Canopy.* Thanks to Travis Meyer and Stacey Tran at Poor Claudia for publishing a selection of this book as the chapbook *Believers* in Fall 2013. "Prism" was included in *Privacy Policy: The Anthology of Surveillance Poetics* (Black Ocean 2014), edited by Andrew Ridker. Lastly, I would be nowhere without the love and support of my mother, father, and sister.

Andrew Durbin co-edits Wonder and lives in New York.

NIGHTBOAT BOOKS

Nightboat Books, a nonprofit organization, seeks to develop audiences for writers whose work resists convention and transcends boundaries. We publish books rich with poignancy, intelligence, and risk. Please visit nightboat.org to learn about our titles and how you can support our future publications.

This book has been made possible by grants from The Fund for Poetry and the New York State Council on the Arts Literature Program. Support was also provided by a Face Out grant, funded by The Jerome Foundation and administered by The Council of Literary Magazines and Presses.